PUTTING COMPUTER POWER IN SCHOOLS:
A Step-by-Step Approach

PUTTING COMPUTER POWER IN SCHOOLS:
A Step-by-Step Approach

Jerry L. Patterson
Janice H. Patterson

PRENTICE-HALL, INC.
Englewood Cliffs, New Jersey

© 1983, *by*

Jerry L. Patterson

Janice H. Patterson

Library of Congress Cataloging in Publication Data

Patterson, Jerry L.
  Putting computer power in schools.

  Bibliography: p.
  Includes index.
  1. Education—Data processing. 2. Computer-assisted
instruction. 3. Microcomputers. I. Patterson,
Janice H. II. Title.
LB1028.43.P37   1983   370′.028′5   83-8017
ISBN 0-13-744474-5

Printed in the United States of America

DEDICATION

To Janna and Jerrod, our legacy to humankind.

ACKNOWLEDGMENTS

This has been an exciting project. Major contributors in the excitement have been our parents and children. Their curiosity, support, and understanding have been our mainstay. Also, we are indebted to our friend and typist, Lois Obrien Opalewski. Without her willing spirit and tolerant heart, we might still be pounding out the pages. She has been superior in meeting short deadlines, producing outstanding work at the same time. Thanks, Lois, for a job well done.

ABOUT THE AUTHORS

Dr. Jerry L. Patterson holds a Ph.D. in Curriculum and Instruction from Ohio University. Currently Assistant Superintendent for instruction with the Madison, Wisconsin, Public Schools, Dr. Patterson has also served as elementary principal, teacher, university lecturer, research and evaluation specialist, and curriculum coordinator. In addition, he serves as consultant to school districts planning to put computer power in schools. He has authored over two dozen publications in the field of education, including several recent articles on the topic of microcomputers in the schools.

Dr. Janice H. Patterson earned a Ph.D. in Curriculum and Instruction from the University of Wisconsin-Madison. She presently serves as Coordinator for Instructional Computing with the Wisconsin Center for Education Research, School of Education, UW-Madison. Formerly a teacher, consultant, and administrator of several projects at UW, Dr. Patterson has published numerous manuscripts in educational journals, plus chapters in a forthcoming book.

PREFACE

Never before in our lifetime has any innovation taken education by storm as much as computer technology. From every segment of the community, telltale signs herald public expectations for computers in education. With the demands growing so rapidly, it's difficult to know which way to turn. At last, however, help is here in *Putting Computer Power in Schools: A Step-by-Step Approach.* Compiled in one comprehensive and practical volume are all the guidelines, step-by-step approaches, and useful hints you need to use computer power effectively in your school. Written in a nontechnical, easy-to-understand style, this book cuts through all the jargon and propaganda to get at the heart of what you need to know about putting computers in schools.

Chapter 1, "Making Sense Out of Confusion: Deciding What's Important to Know About Computers," guides you through the maze of computer terms and concepts in a way that leaves you with a clear understanding of the knowledge needed to be an informed decision-maker and user of computers.

In Chapter 2, "Using Computers as an Aid to Instruction," you get a step-by-step explanation of the important role computers play via Computer Assisted Learning. This chapter describes how you can use computers in a wide variety of subject areas and grade levels, what computers can do better than books, and how you can go about choosing Computer Assisted Learning that is best suited for your particular students.

The third chapter, "Teaching and Learning About Computers," continues to examine the instructional uses of computer technology by taking a careful look at computer literacy. In this chapter, you learn how to unscramble the confusion over what computer literacy means. You also have at your fingertips four specific goals of a computer literacy curriculum, along with two examples of nationally acclaimed models of a computer literacy curriculum.

Chapter 4, "Freeing Teachers of Tedious Tasks: Computer Managed Instruction," pinpoints for you how computer technology can assert its superiority in managing information, leaving you free to spend more time teaching. The chapter includes lots of examples of how the computer can produce individual and group progress reports, diagnose and prescribe instruction, administer student tests, and handle instructional or administrative changes in your program. These and other computerized tasks show how Computer Managed Instruction can put more of the "teach" back in teaching by letting the computer do more of the managing.

Chapter 5, "Tapping the Power of the Computer as Administrative Assistant," introduces you to the wealth of computer applications available in an administrative setting. Numerous illustrations are given of how the computer can be used to save time and money in preparing payroll, student report cards, and schedules, as well as exciting new breakthroughs in word processing. In addition, you receive a comprehensive set of guidelines to help you decide which administrative uses are most important for your situation.

The sixth chapter, "Selecting Computer Applications You Need the Most," guides you, step by step, through this decision-making process. First, you learn how to apply a common set of criteria to each computer application. Next, you follow a carefully designed procedure to decide which computer needs have the highest priority. Throughout Chapter 6, you are given plenty of examples to show how you can make this process work in your own setting.

Chapter 7, "The Right Way to Buy a Computer," uses the decisions you made in earlier chapters to develop a comprehensive procedure for choosing the right computer to fit your needs. A proven process is outlined, with each step carefully explained, leading you to a rational decision regarding the purchase of a computer system. Following the guidelines offered in this chapter, you can buy your computer with confidence and a minimum of confusion.

"Finding the Right Software," the focus of Chapter 8, again takes you step-by-step through tested criteria as you evaluate software. The chapter presents helpful hints and outlines pitfalls to avoid in pursuing quality software. You also get up-to-the-minute advice on the pros and cons of developing your own software.

Chapter 9, "Developing an Action Plan for Implementing Computer Technology," takes the decision-making process one step further by outlining a plan of action for introducing computers in the schools. This chapter draws on both the successes and failures of other schools to give you concrete advice on how to establish a plan of action. You learn four critical factors shaping the quality of implementation, as well as strategies for resolving teacher and administrator concerns about using computers in schools.

The final chapter, "Anticipating the Future," looks to the future by taking the most current thought and practice in computer technology and projecting the continued development of this exciting innovation into the future. This chapter takes a no-nonsense view of what the promise may be for computer capabilities and what the reality of computer use in schools will be during the coming years.

Janice H. Patterson,
Jerry L. Patterson

CONTENTS

tice, 37. Creating Simulated Worlds Via Computer, 38. What the Computer Can Do Better Than Books, 40. Using CAL Throughout the Curriculum, 43. How to Choose the CAL Best Suited to Your Students, 47. Chapter 2 References, 48.

Clarifying the Need to Have a Computer Literacy Curriculum, 51. Unscrambling the Confusion Over Computer Literacy, 52. Proposed Aim of a Computer Literacy Curriculum, 53. Four Program Goals of a Computer Literacy Curriculm, 54. Resolving Critical Issues Before Deciding on a Computer Literacy Curriculum, 58. Two Exemplary Models of a Computer Curriculum, 60. Chapter 3 References, 73.

Assumptions Underlying CMI, 76. Improving Instructional Management with Computer Power, 80. Points to Ponder in Considering a CMI System, 87. CMI in Action: Two Case Studies, 91. Chapter 4 References, 95.

Putting a Management Information System to Work in Schools, 97. Computerizing Student Files, 97. Using an MIS to Manage Business Operations, 98. Managing the Educational Program with the Help of Computers, 101. Using Word Processing to Improve Clerical Efficiency, 111. Things to Think About Before Deciding on Administrative Applications, 114. Chapter 5 References, 117.

About Using Computers, 192. Building Staff
Development into Your Planning Efforts, 195.
Successfully Managing the Implementation of
Computer Technology, 198. Chapter 9 Refer-
ences, 203.

Short-Term Plans vs. Long-Range Planning,
206. Keeping Up with Changes in Hardware,
207. Software of the Future, 210. Tomorrow's
Goals for Computer Technology, 211. The Role
of Computers in Tomorrow's Schools, 216.
Chapter 10 References, 218.

══ MAKING SENSE OUT OF ══ CONFUSION: DECIDING WHAT'S IMPORTANT TO KNOW ABOUT COMPUTERS

For virtually all of us, the introduction of something new in our lives generates a host of concerns about this "new something." In education, we have watched hundreds of so-called innovations come and go. If we had jumped on every bandwagon parading in front of the schoolhouse doors, our entire educational experience could be summarized in one word: chaos. Fortunately, educators have developed highly sensitive "junk detectors." Partly by trial and error, but mainly through our training and experience, we have been able to detect innovations that hold promise as well as those that aren't useful in educating our students.

Now we are faced with a new innovation, the exploding field of computer technology. And now our junk detectors send us mixed messages. On the one hand, we know beyond a doubt that a primary ingredient in any student's learning is the skillful, compassionate guidance of a trained teacher. We also know that a machine can't duplicate the humanistic element found in effective teaching. On the other hand, we see, hear, and read more about this thing called computer technology than any other innovation in recent memory. The topic of computers has taken our profession by storm. The community is beginning to ask tough questions about the place of computers in schools and classrooms. Even kids are getting into the act; they are talking about *RAM, Bytes, Floppy Disks*, and other strange-sounding words. We are caught in a tug-of-war, being pushed into exploring an innovation we know very little about and being pulled by the strength of our own professional experience, which tells us not to be too hasty about jumping on the innovation bandwagon.

A basic purpose of this book is to help you satisfactorily work through this dilemma. *Putting Computer Power in Schools* acknowledges the indispensable role you and other professional educators play in our schools, and, at the same time, takes a realistic view of what the field of computer technology can contribute toward improving the quality of education. So this is not a book written to promote the uncontrolled proliferation of computers in every nook and cranny of every classroom. It is written to provide you with a clearer understanding of the capabilities and limitations of computer technology. More importantly, however, it is written as your guide to effectively using computers in schools.

REMOVING THE JARGON
FROM COMPUTER LANGUAGE

It's easy to be intimidated by the jargon thrown around in computer circles. But once you can cut through the shorthand, you will find that the concepts aren't difficult to understand. Even though you don't need a course on computers, you do need a reference guide to translate computer jargon into plain English. Figure 1-1 offers a framework to help accomplish this.

FIGURE 1-1. COMPUTER GLOSSARY

BASIC: An acronym for Beginner's All-purpose Symbolic Instruction Code. This is a computer language used extensively in computer programs written for education. Many introductory courses in computer programming teach BASIC.

BUG: An error. If you have a bug in your program, you need to correct it so the program will work properly.

BYTE: The space in a computer needed to store one character such as a number, letter, or other symbol.

CENTRAL PROCESSING UNIT (CPU): The part of the computer that stores and carries out the instructions given by the computer program. The CPU of a middle-priced computer system can process several million instructions per second.

CHARACTER: Any letter, number or other symbol that a computer uses in the handling of information. The letter *a* and the number 3 would be examples of characters.

CHIP: A small piece of silicon containing thousands of electric "switches" controlling the processing of information in a computer. Sometimes this is referred to as a microprocessor chip.

COMPUTER LANGUAGE: A special set of words and grammatical rules used to write instructions for a computer to carry out. Some names given to these languages are BASIC, COBOL, LOGO and PASCAL.

COURSEWARE: Computer programs designed specifically for use in educational settings. In other words, it is software for courses.

CURSOR: A lighted or blinking symbol on a computer screen marking the next spot where information will appear when entered as input.

DATA: Information to be used by the computer.

DISK DRIVE: A machine connected to the computer that can store and get information from a disk.

FLOPPY DISK: A plastic disk, about the size of a 45 r.p.m. record, on which many pages of information (including computer programs) can be stored. Sometimes this is simply called a disk.

FLOWCHART: A diagram used to plot the step-by-step instructions necessary to accomplish a specific task. Frequently flowcharts are used to outline the steps in a computer program.

HARDWARE: All of the equipment that makes up a computer system, including input, output, storage, and processing devices.

INPUT: The information given to a computer from an input device.

INPUT DEVICE: Equipment used for putting information into a computer. A common input device is the keyboard.

KILOBYTE: Literally, 1024 bytes. Many times the computing power of a machine is referred to as 16K, 48K, 256K, etc. A 48K computer, for instance, has space to store over 48,000 characters of information, or about 30 double-spaced, typewritten pages.

MODEM: An abbreviation for Modulator-DEModulator. It is a device that allows information to pass from one computer to another (or to a terminal) over telephone lines.

PERIPHERAL: Any add-on device to a computer that can transfer information to and from the computer. Examples of peripherals include printers, cassette recorders, and modems.

PROGRAM: A set of step-by-step instructions, written in a computer language, telling the computer to perform an identified task or series of tasks.

RANDOM ACCESS MEMORY (RAM): The amount of space inside the computer that can be used for storing information transferred from a device outside the computer. Thirty-two K of RAM provides for the storage of over 32,000 bytes (characters) of information transferred into the machine.

READ ONLY MEMORY (ROM): The amount of information built into the computer at the factory. This permanent memory contains instructions telling the computer how to follow directions given by the person operating the machine.

SOFTWARE: Essentially the programs used to operate a computer. This information can be entered through input devices such as the keyboard, or stored on devices such as a cassette recorder and disk drive.

After learning this vocabulary, you should be in a position to carry on a conversation with a computer buff, at least on a topic pertaining to the world of schools. In the technical world of computer science, many more peculiar-sounding words exist. If one of these terms pops up in a conversation, simply say, "Can you tell me what that means in regular language?" Many computer specialists don't intentionally try to be obscure, and they do want to communicate clearly to teachers and administrators. Sometimes they just need a little reminder.

COMMUNICATING WITH THE COMPUTER

Much of the apprehension about computers comes from not knowing how they handle information. Actually a basic communication model, as shown in Figure 1-2, can be used to explain how to communicate with a computer. This model can be applied to anything from typewriters to calculators to computers. Let's look at each one of these in turn.

FIGURE 1-2. BASIC COMMUNICATION MODEL

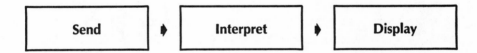

| Send | | Interpret | | Display |

Sending a message by typewriter consists of the sender selecting the information to be communicated, entering the message on the keyboard, and observing the message being displayed on the typing paper. In this case, no interpretation of the information takes place. The input device, the keyboard, is linked directly to the output device, the typewriter keys. The receiver gets the information exactly as typed by the sender.

Processing information with the calculator follows the same model. The sender enters the information (input) onto a keyboard, which is then sent electronically to an interpreter within the calculator. In computer jargon, this interpreter is called a micro-processor chip. The chip has been designed with a set of instructions to follow, depending on the specific information entered by the sender. Suppose, for example, the sender entered 3 × 4 on the keyboard. The chip has been instructed to carry out the instructions and convey the results in the form of an answer shown in the display window of the calculator. Communicating with a calculator differs in one important way from doing so with a typewriter. The calculator has the capability of acting on the information put into the machine in order to produce the results the sender asked for. But the calculator can only perform one set of instructions at a time. You can't tell the calculator to multiply a set of four problems all at once. Additional capabilities are needed for following multiple instructions.

This is where the computer steps in. Even though the computer offers advantages over the conventional typewriter and calculator for some purposes, it follows the same basic model: send, interpret, and display information. The sender enters information as input into the machine. The microprocessor chip interprets the information and displays it in a form understood by the receiver of the message.

A major distinction between the computer and other information processing devices is the computer's ability to carry out a series of steps at once, and to do so with great speed. As an example, the computer can do more arithmetic in one minute than a person using paper and pencil can do in a lifetime. Even with its speed, accuracy, and ability to follow complicated, detailed sets of instructions, the computer operates on the same principles as the familiar typewriter and calculator. If this is the case, why is there such an aura of mystery, suspicion, and downright intimidation created by the possibility of computers in schools? A big part of the answer lies in our lack of knowledge about how computers work.

EXPLAINING IN PLAIN LANGUAGE
HOW COMPUTERS WORK

Now that you have a general understanding of how computers process information, let's look at a more detailed description of how computers work, including the jargon and what it really means in familiar terms.

First of all, it is important to distinguish between the major categories of computers. For our purposes they can be grouped as:

- mainframe computers
- minicomputers
- computer terminals
- microcomputers
- hand-held computers

Back in the old days (less than twenty years ago), most computing power came from the physically massive computers handling the computerized data processing of large-scale operations such as government agencies and school districts. A step down from the big "mainframe" computer is the minicomputer, having many of the characteristics of its larger scale relative, but with less computing power. One of the first entries into schools was made by the computer terminal. These machines serve as an extension to the main computer. In fact, terminals usually have a telephone hookup (called a modem), and the communication between terminal and computer occurs over the phone lines. With the invention of the microprocessor chip (the part mentioned earlier that can do calculations), we saw the arrival of the microcomputer. Because of its portability, versatility, and low cost, this machine will be the dominant computer in homes and schools for the next several years. Growing in popularity is the hand-held computer. As computing capabilities increase and prices decrease, hand-held computers will find a place in schools. For the purpose of this book, however, most references to the term "computer" will actually mean the microcomputer.

For a basic understanding of how computers work, you should be familiar with five parts of a computing system, diagrammed in Figure 1-3:

- input devices
- Central Processing Unit
- memory storage in the computer
- memory storage outside the computer
- output devices

Each of these is carefully explained on pages 22–24.

FIGURE 1-3. COMPONENTS OF A COMPUTING SYSTEM

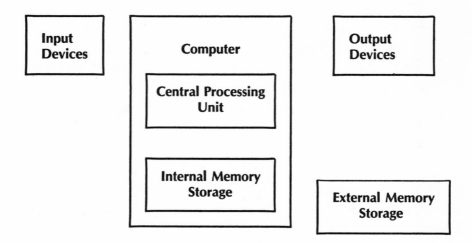

Input Devices

An input device is any piece of equipment that puts information into the computer. The most common form is the standard typewriter keyboard. Other ways to send information are by light pen, graphics tablet, and voice. Since these devices aren't the usual means for communicating with the computer, a description of their function will be saved for later.

Central Processing Unit (CPU)

When computer buffs refer to the CPU, they mean the space inside the computer that does the processing of information entered through the keyboard. Sometimes called the "brain" of the computer, the main part of this unit is the microprocessor chip, a small rectangle of silicon about the size of a dime. The chip, which packs more capabilities than older computers large enough to fill a classroom, consists of thousands of "switches" that receive electric impulses. As the electricity flows through the chip, it detects whether each switch is on or off. And, as incredible as this sounds, understanding on and off is the limit of the computer's thinking power. The Central Processing Unit takes the information sent to it and translates the information into a form understood by the machine. This form, called machine language, is made up of only two symbols, 1 and 0. Anything we input into the machine can be changed by the CPU to a 1 (switch turned on) or a 0 (switch turned off). Each number and letter, as well as other symbols, has a distinct code made up of ones and zeros.

Memory Storage Inside the Computer

The computer has space designated inside it for storing information. The permanent memory put in at the factory is called Read Only Memory (ROM). The information in ROM contains a series of instructions telling the computer how to follow directions supplied by the person using the machine. Each brand of computer has its own set of instructions for handling information. A second, more frequently discussed form of memory, is Random Access Memory (RAM). What it really means is the amount of space inside the computer that can be used for storing information transferred from devices outside the computer.

The amount of RAM a computer can hold is measured by how many thousands of characters (letters, symbols, and so on) the machine has space for. Most often, this available space is measured in kilobytes. One kilobyte equals about 1,000 bytes, or 1,000 characters worth of information. To make things clearer, suppose that a certain computer could hold 32,000 characters in storage. In computer jargon, you would say the computer has 32K worth of memory. That is, the computer has the capacity to hold 32,000 characters inside it.

To summarize, if you hear someone say, "Our school's computer has 48 bytes of RAM," what this really means in plain terms is that the computer has room to store about 48,000 characters transferred from another source into the computer. Assuming that, on the average, each typewritten page contained 250 words, a computer with 48K of memory could hold about 30 double-spaced pages of typewritten information at any given time.

Output Devices

The information put in the computer and interpreted by the machine is presented in final form by an output device, usually resembling a TV screen. This screen sometimes is referred to as a video screen, monitor, cathode ray tube (CRT), and other specialized terms. By whatever name, the output devices are necessary for displaying the results of your work in a clear, readable way. Other devices for receiving output include printers, cassette tapes, and disks.

Memory Storage Outside the Computer

Earlier in the chapter, we described how to put symbols into the computer from the keyboard. This turns out to be slow and cumbersome, however, when certain computer programs (instructions telling the computer what to do), prepared reports, or other lengthy documents need to be stored in the computer. A faster, easier way to transfer this information is through the use of equipment specifically designed for storing and transferring large amounts of information. One form of memory storage located outside the computer is the cassette recorder. Information is stored and retrieved by cassette tapes, similar to the ones we use for recording music, speeches, and so on. This method is relatively inexpensive. A much faster, but more expensive way to store information outside the computer is on a disk drive. Operating somewhat like a record player, a disk drive keeps information on something called a floppy disk. This piece of soft "floppy" plastic resembles a smaller version of a 45 r.p.m. record, and works in much the same way. The disk drive goes directly to the spot on the disk where the information is kept, without having to wind serially through all preceding information the way the cassette recorder does. You will find both disk drives and cassette recorders as storage devices for computers used in schools.

The previous discussion has provided you with a basic framework for understanding how computers work. There is more to be learned, but you are now on your way to becoming a computer user.

DO TEACHERS NEED
TO BE COMPUTER PROGRAMMERS?

Now that you've overcome the language barrier and you've made it through a primer on how computers work, you have to deal with the issue of becoming skilled at writing programs. At this point, the technology of computer programming is changing as fast as the machinery itself. In the early 1980s, most of the computer programs for schools were written in the computer language called BASIC (another acronym, Beginners All-purpose Symbolic Instruction Code). The BASIC language, readily learned by both adults and students, typifies how computers "think." That is, computers can perform only after receiving clearly written, logical, step-by-step instructions. Learning the language requires patience, practice, and more practice. You can read a book on how to write computer programs in BASIC, understand the concepts involved, and still have considerable difficulty in getting a computer program to work; that is, do what you want done. The realization that understanding BASIC is not the same as successfully using BASIC raises a critical question. Do teachers and administrators need to be proficient in computer programming to be proficient at teaching about and with computers?

The answer is: it depends. It depends on how you want to use the computer in your classroom. If you plan to introduce the idea of computers and how to run already written programs, programming skills aren't critical. But if you plan to emphasize computer literacy as a skill, clearly you should demonstrate the skill as well. To restate the point, you can provide meaningful student experiences in the area of computer technology without a lot of programming skill. So lack of training in writing programs should not be a deterrent to its use in the classrooms. A final reason for not trying to make all computer users skilled computer programmers lies with the progress made in communicating to computers. Advances in voice recognition capabilities of computers, along with improved computer languages, must be weighed when deciding the level of programming skills necessary for your purposes.

However, the experience of writing even 8- to 10-line computer programs does enable you to understand the basic logical operations required for the computer to follow directions. Sometimes this experience takes the form of drawing flowcharts showing a task's chain of events from start to finish. Even listing in narrative style the series of steps for solving a problem can be helpful to understanding the logic of computer programming. If necessary, then, someone with programming skills can take your information and translate it into language understood by the computer.

So far, in this chapter, we have focused a lot of attention on deciding what's important to know about computers. You may have the impression that everyone thinks computers are the answer to all of education's problems. That's not the whole picture.

FOUR GOOD REASONS NOT TO USE COMPUTERS

Because computer technology is still in its infancy, many important questions regarding its usefulness have yet to be answered. Four of the most frequent reasons for not using computers in schools are outlined below.

Passing Fad

Plenty of evidence in the parade of innovations passing through the schools never make it through the classroom door. In some respects, this is healthy. Classroom teachers and administrators need to use their filters for separating the trivial and cosmetic from innovations that hold real promise. In the case of computers in schools, the innovation has all the markings associated with other bandwagon, new-fangled ideas: community excitement, extensive media coverage, big promises of things to come. A major difference between computer technology and many other so-called innovations preceding it is the unknown potential of computers. Those who yell "fad" are asked to withhold judgment until we know more about what computers can do in schools.

No More Energy to Spend

Everything from official polls to informal conversations confirms that today's educators are taxed more than ever. Not only are teachers expected to teach the basics; basics are more broadly defined and includes topics like interpersonal relations, fine arts, driver's education, sex education, and the list goes on. According to some teachers, adding computers to the list will require an expenditure of more energy, a commodity already in short supply. The mere thought of tackling a new priority leaves teachers tired.

Unproven Cost-Effectiveness

Although the cost of computers has dropped markedly in the last few years, the price tag still looks large in the face of dwindling school resources. And the price of the computer doesn't reflect the cost of the entire unit, consisting of storage devices, display screen, plus other accessories. When considering a high-cost item like computers for classrooms, you also have to consider what you are getting as a return on your investment. Quite frankly, we don't have a long line of research showing precisely how computers can be used most effectively in schools. While researchers point to some academic gains when computers serve as instructional aids, classroom teachers ask rather bluntly, "In the average classroom, what can the computer do more effectively than I'm doing right now?"

Lack of Administrative Support

As with all innovations, there is a core of teachers who have assumed the initiative and caused exciting things to happen with computers in the classroom. These early users have been creative in their efforts to get funds, develop programs, and sell parents and kids on the virtues of computer technology. Once the initial excitement moderates, many of these teachers realize they have little administrative support for program continuity, much less program expansion. Faced with competing priorities, school district officials find themselves in a dilemma: while they initially encouraged these innovative teachers to explore the capabilities of computers in the classroom, the decision-makers find it difficult to support additional program efforts, especially if a price tag is attached. In some instances, teachers have not been able to secure principal endorsement for teaching with and about computers in the classroom. When this support base doesn't seem apparent, the computer advocate may respond, "Why bother?"

FOUR BETTER REASONS
FOR USING COMPUTERS IN SCHOOLS

Despite the valid reservations about jumping hastily onto the computer bandwagon, both research evidence and current practice point to some strong reasons for using computers in schools.

Computer-Assisted Learning (CAL)

At the outset, it should be stated clearly that computers never will replace teachers. Human interchange can't be duplicated by computers. These machines have no emotions; they have no capability for intimate interaction so crucial to the social and emotional development of children. Try to imagine, for instance, a twelve-year-old discussing with the computer-as-counselor why the student cries easily when her friends poke fun at her clothes, tease her about her weight, and laugh at her clumsiness in gym class. Granting the teacher's primary role in education, also imagine a computer that can give a student as much practice as necessary on mathematics facts without tiring, without registering impatience, and with the capability of changing the questions depending on the student's progress. Imagine, too, a student being able to conduct a "dangerous" science experiment of mixing volatile chemicals in the safe environment of a simulated science lab displayed on the computer screen. Other examples of Computer Assisted Learning include: composing stories on the computer, then applying the text-editing capability of writing, deleting, rearranging, and so on, all without having to "rewrite" additional drafts; using the sound and graphics capabilities of computers to teach handicapped students; engaging students in creative problem-solving, using interactive dialogue leading to various solutions, depending on the student's response pattern. These and many other approaches to using the computer as an instructional aid will be explored in Chapter 2. For now it is sufficient to underscore that computers can be an invaluable resource to the learning process without usurping the role rightfully held by the most significant influence in a child's school life—the classroom teacher.

Computer Literacy

Regardless of any philosophical preference we may hold, our children and their children will live in a highly technological society far beyond our wildest imagination. The development of computer technology is still in the embryonic stage. Just around the corner is a world of electronic cash, electronic mail, computerized wrist phones, as well as electronic classrooms where each child has his or her own computer module built into each desk. These aren't idle speculations; they have a high probability of taking shape relatively soon. Improved computer technology, in fields such as medicine, industrial production, and transportation, will revolutionize the way we live. As students take their place, our place, in the world of the future, they deserve to assume their various positions with a solid understanding of computer technology. As educators, we assume a major responsibility for seeing that this understanding occurs. Schools must give attention to computer literacy in the curriculum. Chapter 3 takes you step-by-step through the tasks necessary to accomplish this.

Computer-Managed Instruction (CMI)

Most teachers and administrators rally to the cry of reducing tedious paperwork and other tasks interfering with instruction. As discussed in Chapter 4, computers have come to the assistance of teachers in managing such tasks as recordkeeping, scoring tests, and keeping track of students' academic progress. With the computer asserting its qualities of speed, accuracy, and reliability in the handling of routine management tasks normally consuming much of the teacher's time, more time becomes available for the student.

Computer as Administrative Assistant

The management skills of the computer can be applied in the office environment as well as the classroom. The incredible speed and accuracy of computers are currently being used in school offices to handle payroll, develop budget projections and status reports, create efficient bus routes, schedule classes, drastically cut secretarial time in word processing, and to perform other tasks individually tailored to each administrator's needs. In this era when new knowledge is exploding at exponential rates, computer assistance in the management of data provides welcome relief. The business community moved sooner than education to make administrative applications of computers, but we have quickened our pace. In the near future, both administrators and secretaries will find the computer as indispensable as the typewriter and telephone. Chapter 5 presents in detail how this will probably happen.

Weighing the evidence, computers certainly deserve a place in our schools. The concerns expressed earlier are real, however. They need to be dealt with in a thoughtful, problem-solving mode. But we can rise above these barriers and pave the way for the smooth arrival of computers in the classroom. No one can say with precision what role computers should play when they enter the schools, or what the future holds for this technology as it continues to mature. Several things seem clear, however. As teachers and administrators, we have an obligation to demonstrate a basic knowledge of how computers work, make reasoned decisions about appropriate applications in our schools, and develop a sound plan of action for adopting and implementing computer technology. Chapter 1 has laid the groundwork for understanding in general terms what the computer can and can't do. The balance of the book takes you through the steps of how you can effectively use computers in the applications that are most important to you.

CHAPTER 1 REFERENCES

Coburn, P., P. Kelman, N. Roberts, T. Snyder, D. Watt, and C. Weiner, *Practical Guide to Computers in Education*, Reading, MA: Addison-Wesley, 1982.

Moursund, D., *Introduction to Computers in Education for Elementary and Middle School Teachers*, Eugene, OR: International Council for Computers in Education, 1981.

Moursund, D., *School Administrator's Introduction to Instructional Use of Computers*, Eugene, OR: International Council for Computers in Education, 1980.

Papert, S., *Mindstorms: Children, Computers and Powerful Ideas*, New York, NY: Basic Books, 1980.

USING COMPUTERS AS AN AID TO INSTRUCTION

Today, as in the past, most classrooms consist of the teacher as central figure, with twenty to thirty students per class. Now, however, we are faced with the emergence of another model, one that includes computer technology in addition to the teacher. The availability of the computer as a teaching assistant means that we might have to alter our former ways of operating in the classroom. The prospect of such changes raises a series of legitimate questions asked by the classroom teacher, such as: Will the computer be more trouble than it is worth? How will the kids respond? Can the computer really help my teaching? What are the advantages, if any, of computers over textbooks? The purpose of this chapter is to respond to these and other related questions through a description of Computer Assisted Learning (CAL).

EXPLAINING THE ROLE OF CAL IN THE CLASSROOM

Before examining the role of computers in the classroom, we first need to clarify some other computer jargon. Various labels identify the computer as an assistant in the learning process, the most frequent title being Computer Assisted Instruction (CAI). In practice, CAI has about a twenty-year track record in the schools. While these early attempts were noble, many of the CAI programs lacked the sophistication in design found in today's programs. In discussing contemporary programs that focus on learning with the help of computers, this book uses the term Computer Assisted Learning (CAL) because CAL places the emphasis on learning, the ultimate goal of teaching. Also, it distinguishes the recent efforts at learning via computers from earlier attempts.

Returning to the main point, in order to examine the appropriate place for computers in the classroom, we need to look at the various purposes of teaching a lesson, which range from the simplistic to the overly complex. To keep things concise and straightforward, we will discuss only three basic purposes of instruction such as:

- understanding new material
- reviewing material already taught
- applying learned material to problems, issues, situations, and so on

Material, in this context, can mean knowledge, skills, attitudes, or other objectives considered important by the classroom teacher. The next three sections will help you decide the most suitable CAL strategy, based on the specific purposes of instruction.

LETTING THE COMPUTER SERVE AS TUTOR

For teaching new material to an individual or a small group of students, the computer makes an excellent tutor. The tutorial mode, consisting of dialog between computer and student, is illustrated in Figure 2-1. Not all CAL programs contain this exact

FIGURE 2-1. COMPUTER ASSISTED LEARNING DIALOG

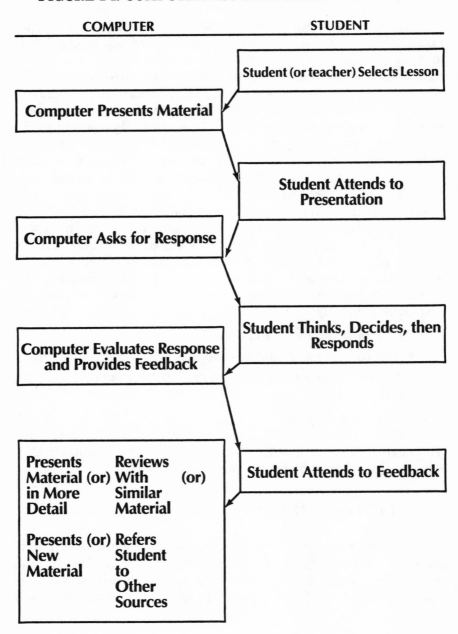

sequence. Modifications are made to fit the particular purpose of teaching and the needs of the student participating in the CAL dialog.

To show how the computer can tutor, let's trace a hypothetical lesson through the CAL sequence described above. (*See* Gagné et al., 1981.) Assume that the learning objective for this lesson is to correctly identify figures that are parallelograms. Let's see how the dialog might develop between the computer and the student we'll call Marge.

Student Selects Lesson

Marge turns on the computer and goes through the necessary steps to have the first part of the lesson appear on the screen.

Computer Presents Material

The computer gains Marge's attention by first flashing colorful geometric shapes on the screen, then rapidly drawing shapes in various sizes. Unfortunately, this can't be shown in a book. Next the computer engages in the following dialog:

"This lesson teaches you to identify figures that are parallelograms. Remember, we have already talked about the concepts of straight lines, polygons, and quadrilaterals. If you need more review on this before we move on, hit the RETURN key."

Then the computer continues the lesson by slowly drawing an outline of five parallelograms, one at a time, with the explanation:

"Each of these is a parallelogram."

In a similar way, the computer draws three shapes that aren't parallelograms and explains why they aren't.

Student Attends to Presentation

Although this statement may seem self-evident, it's important to underscore the fact that a CAL lesson involves constant interaction between the computer and the student. Up to this point, the computer is actively teaching via presentation of new material, and Marge is actively engaged by paying attention to the tutor.

Computer Asks for Response

After the initial presentation, the computer presents eight figures, appropriately labeled 1 through 8, and says:
"Type each number that labels a parallelogram."
Depending on the purpose of instruction, questioning by the computer can range from mere recall to challenging the student to apply the material in a new context.

Student Thinks, Decides, then Responds

At this stage in the dialog, Marge takes a more active role. She uses the information presented in the lesson, as well as knowledge gained from prior lessons, to formulate a response to the computer's query. In this case, the response takes the form of selecting from a list of choices displayed on the screen. In other instances, Marge might respond by drawing shapes on the screen with a special device called a light pen, or by typing in phrases the computer compares to a master list of acceptable answers stored in memory.

Computer Evaluates Response and Provides Feedback

Most CAL lessons make it possible for the computer to evaluate the student's response and provide helpful feedback about what to do next. In the dialog with Marge, the computer shows Marge all the correct responses and informs her:
"You correctly identified all three of the parallelograms, but you incorrectly identified two figures as parallelograms."
Analyzing her responses, the computer finds that each of her incorrect responses contained four sides like a parallelogram, but contained sides of unequal lengths.

Student Attends to Feedback

Now it is Marge's turn to take action in the dialog. She considers the feedback offered by the computer, then decides among the following options what she wants the computer to do next:

- Present the same material again.
- Present new material.
- Review similar material.
- Give a quiz on the current material.
- Refer the student to other sources for further study.

In our hypothetical lesson, Marge decides she wants to see the same material again because she isn't satisfied with her performance.

Computer Presents Additional Material

At this juncture, the computer receives Marge's choice and proceeds accordingly. This capability to choose among a variety of paths, or "branches" in computer jargon, is an important part of learning in the tutorial mode. Each time the CAL sequence starts over, the dialog can develop in various ways, depending on the nature of each individual student's response pattern.

The hypothetical dialog between Marge and the computer represents a brief snapshot of how CAL in the tutorial mode takes place when the purpose of instruction is to understand new material. In actual classroom settings, typical dialogs are much more complex, involving a more extended interaction between tutor and tutee. Nevertheless, this example illustrates, on a small scale, what can happen when the computer and the student team up in a teaching-learning situation.

LETTING THE COMPUTER
CONDUCT DRILL AND PRACTICE

With over twenty students at once in a typical classroom, the teacher finds it difficult to provide individualized help for students who need it. And usually such practice takes different forms, depending on what each learner had difficulty with when the material was first presented. Enter the computer with its patient, untiring, and systematic approach to drill and practice. The teaching sequence involved in drill and practice represents a modification of the tutorial CAL dialog model discussed earlier. When the basic purpose of instruction is to review material already taught, the computer limits the options available to the student. For example, if Marge is having difficulty understanding the concept of parallelograms, she may not have the choice to move on to new material or take a quiz on the current material. Instead, based on the computer's evaluation of Marge's response pattern in the dialog, the computer may decide Marge needs a lot more practice. So the dialog takes the form of displaying sets of figures and asking Marge to identify parallelograms. Again, using Marge's response as the basis for its judgment, the computer determines if the drill is improving her performance. If not, the computer may decide to use an alternative technique to teach the concepts involved in the lesson. Once Marge shows she understands the concept by correctly identifying the parallelograms, the computer may give the student more practice by presenting several multi-shaped objects and asking Marge to pick out all the parallelogram shapes. Imagine how time-consuming it would be for the class-room teacher to construct such drill and practice lessons, tailoring each one to the needs of the individual student.

Before leaving the idea of drill and practice, it should be pointed out that poorly designed lessons of this type are not worth using. If the CAL program doesn't offer options based on the students' needs and concentrates solely on giving students the equivalent of pages of problems without any instruction, the teacher may be better off relying on the conventional workbook. With this as a caveat, however, the teacher can expect the computer to be an excellent helper in classroom drill and practice.

CREATING SIMULATED WORLDS VIA COMPUTER

Another purpose of instruction is to apply material already learned to new situations, problems, issues, and so on. The computer has long been regarded as a powerful tool for achieving this purpose. One of the most exciting instructional applications of computer technology is in the field of simulations. Stepping outside the classroom for a moment, consider how computer simulations have been used in training aircraft pilots. Situations are created whereby aspiring pilots experience vicariously on the screen actual flight conditions. Decisions made and maneuvers attempted during this simulated flight can be analyzed and reported by the computer, even to the extreme case in which the aircraft crashes and no survivors are reported.

Stepping back inside the classroom, imagine the variety of situations calling for the student to experiment with risk-taking activities without actually taking any personal risks. In the chemistry lab, for instance, students can mix volatile chemicals in safety. In science class, the teacher can have the students participate in critical decision-making during a nuclear power plant crisis. The effects of human decisions, including possible errors in judgment, can be studied without actual threat to our planet. These examples just scratch the surface of how simulations can be applied to teaching things considered too "dangerous" for students to experience firsthand.

Another form of simulation is called "the limited world." In other words, it's possible for the computer to present worlds for students to experience, while controlling the conditions of this world. As an illustration, suppose you wanted students to develop skills in reading maps. A motivational way to teach this concept is to have students "experience" being in the middle of a city with a map in hand. With the help of the computer screen, the students could be in downtown Chicago; they could see the buildings, landmarks, and street signs. The students' assignment is to get to a particular destination in the city. As they travel through the city, the students can stop the computer at any intersection and choose to turn left, right or proceed straight ahead. Their trip can be timed, creating an incentive to take the shortest route possible to their destination. A variation of this lesson could let students operate an emergency vehicle so they could move along their route as rapidly as possible. The computer's capability of creating this controllable world adds a dimension to learning not easily achieved through other modes of instruction.

Another type of simulation allows students to solve problems foreign to their everyday world. For instance, a CAL lesson can simulate an international conference addressing the issue of world hunger. Students can study the various data delivered at the conference, and then make decisions based on these data. Finally, the students' conclusions can be compared to those of the "real" experts, with explanations of any discrepancies between the two sets of opinions. These illustrations are representative of how the CAL dialog model described earlier invites interaction through simulations and other methods of problem solving. The computer's capability to make this type of learning possible should prove a valuable aid to the classroom teacher.

WHAT THE COMPUTER CAN DO BETTER THAN BOOKS

So far, this chapter has emphasized how the computer can serve as tutor, hold review sessions with students, and present simulated environments for students to experience. In its aim to help students learn, the computer sometimes finds itself in direct competition with textbooks. Even though textbooks will continue to be the dominant medium for delivering instruction in the near future, the computer offers several features conducive to learning not readily found in textbooks.

Sound

From the attention-getting novelty of bells and whistles, to the sophisticated use of computerized speech, sound adds a dimension to CAL that students seem to like. One of the most frequent applications of sound in CAL programs is the fanfare greeting students' correct responses. In a similar way, music is interspersed throughout programs to call attention to particular responses and to embellish the lesson with a little variety. In some CAL programs, the embellishment borders on the obnoxious. Still, used wisely, sound creates a more interesting lesson. In fact, computerized speech is integral to some CAL programs. For instance, several commercial CAL packages are designed so the computer gives students spelling words. After hearing the word, students type a response into the computer, which in turn assesses the accuracy of the word spelled. Other examples of employing sound features are CAL lessons designed to teach pitch, rhythm, and melody. Clearly, sound is one dimension in learning that can't be duplicated by textbooks.

Color

Although color occasionally is found in printed classroom materials, the production costs of adding color prohibit its liberal use. On the other hand, computers with color features can use this capability at will and at no additional cost. Advertising companies are quick to point out the virtues of color for gaining and holding the attention of the audience. Certainly, the overwhelming majority of families choose color TVs over black and white ones. In the field of computer technology, several reasons exist for incorporating color into CAL lessons. For one thing, it serves as a motivational device. Many elementary school children enjoy creating colorful patterns on the screen through simple programs. Color images are more pleasing visually. This is clearly illustrated when observing student reactions to black and white versus color computer screens. Color can also be used for emphasizing points, particularly for highlighting similarities and differences in the material on the screen. In summary, the judicious use of color in CAL can yield results not easily produced through the printed medium.

Graphics

One of the most fascinating aspects of CAL is the computer's ability to use graphics in the teaching-learning process. While books, like computers, have the capacity to use graphics in the form of pictorial information, the computer combines the concepts of graphics and motion to represent material in a dynamic, rather than static mode. Whether you are teaching the Piagetian concept of conservation by pouring liquid from one container to another, right in front of students' eyes, or plotting a mathematical function students can see developing on the screen, graphics definitely complement printed material in CAL lessons.

Interactive Learning

Without question, a very powerful feature of CAL programs is the interactive dialog between computer and student. As described earlier in the chapter, the student takes an active part in the learning process set up by CAL. Sometimes the computer dominates the interaction, but often the student is the one selecting a particular lesson from a range of choices, acting on the material presented by the computer, and forming judgments, theories, or attitudes based on the CAL lesson. This type of dialog is unachievable from reading a textbook.

Individualized Teaching

As educators, if we value the uniqueness of each student as an individual, and if we believe in the goal of tailoring instruction to the needs of each individual, we find ourselves struggling to individualize instruction. One of the first attempts by publishers to individualize instructional materials came in the form of programmed learning texts. Based on stimulus-response learning theory, these materials were designed so that students moved through the instructional sequence according to somewhat of a fixed pattern. The major distinction between this form of teaching and the current CAL programs is the lack of individualization under the programmed text format. That is, all students were presented the same material, except those who got to skip some of the frames. In Computer Assisted Learning, the students choose how they want to proceed through a lesson. As evident from the example involving Marge and the computer, CAL lessons don't necessarily lock each student into a single pattern of learning. Rather, the lesson can be individualized to fit the needs of the students. Even though individualization has long been a goal of classroom teachers, quality CAL programs offer a level of individualization not easily reached by the textbook alone.

Student Control Over Rate of Presentation

In the conventional textbook presentation, material is printed on the page in the same way for all students. Sometimes the amount of stimuli on one page proves overwhelming and interferes with learning. Students have little choice regarding the amount of material presented at one time.

In CAL lessons, the computer program can be written so that only small segments of the lesson appear on the screen at any given time. Additionally, the material can be presented in a way that combines the most effective use of text and screen space. As the material appears, the students exercise control over how long it stays on display. In other words, students don't have to move on to other material in the lesson until they feel ready to do so. Unlike working with textbooks, the students control the pace of learning by controlling the flow of material presented.

Obviously not all of the advantages cited above are available on all computers or written into all CAL programs. For instance, some computers don't have color capabilities; some CAL programs present a lesson without individualizing any of it. However, the point of this section is to highlight areas where the computer has the capability of supplementing textbooks in the overall learning process.

USING CAL THROUGHOUT THE CURRICULUM

On the surface, some subject areas seem to be better suited than others to using CAL. The purpose of this section is to briefly call attention to a range of CAL applications available for your school's consideration.

Mathematics

Perhaps the most conspicuous place to look for CAL in action is in the math curriculum. With its emphasis on problem solving and logic, mathematics represents a "natural" spot to start using computers. In fact, mathematics educators find themselves in a position of having to explain why computers end up in the math class and not in other classrooms. Also, because mathematics tends to have clearly defined and easily measured objectives, the discipline can easily be adapted to a CAL program. In mathematics, the most frequent application of CAL is in drill and practice. The computer is particularly suited to mastery learning in which students must spend a lot of time practicing fundamentals such as multiplication and division. The computer can guide this practice in varied and entertaining ways, without registering the frustrations that teachers sometimes experience. Plenty of resources and exemplary programs exist for teachers and administrators interested in using CAL to teach these and other concepts.

Science

In a related way, science is an area well suited to CAL. Inherent in the scientific method is a logical, step-by-step approach to solving problems. Much of the CAL applications in science are located in the science classes at the high school level. Particularly popular is CAL via simulation of experimental laboratory conditions. Teachers can set up a laboratory simply by selecting a computer program. They don't have to spend time actually getting the equipment, arranging all of the materials, developing the instructions, supervising the experiment, and then having to clean up the lab after the experiment. For instance, students can carry out the steps necessary to analyze solutions for their acidic or alkaline content; all of these steps can be performed within the lab simulated by the computer. After the experiment, the laboratory can be dismantled simply by turning off the computer. Having a broad range of simulated conditions and limited worlds within their reach, science educators can justify the expense of bringing Computer Assisted Learning into the classroom.

Social Studies

The social studies curriculum can be fertile ground for CAL. One goal of the social studies is to prepare students for participation in a highly technological world. Therefore, social scientists agree that computers should be in social studies classes so students can get hands-on experience using them. Another goal of the social studies is to develop decision-making skills. CAL, in the form of the limited world simulation, has been used in developing this skill. Examples of simulation in social studies classes include:

- an international conference on the nuclear arms race
- a mock election, complete with candidates' positions and political funds to be spent
- a courtroom proceeding in which the student, as judge, weighs the evidence and reaches a verdict
- a conference on economics, where important decisions need to be made about regulating the nation's money supply

These examples illustrate the wealth of learning that could occur through CAL applied to the social studies curriculum.

Language Arts

One of the fastest growing areas for CAL is the language arts curriculum. Computer programs have existed for a long time on the topic of spelling. More recently, though, teachers are discovering that the features of CAL are excellent for teaching students composition skills. Asserting its ability to change, delete, and insert text with the touch of a key, the computer holds promise for teaching students necessary skills of composing, editing, and writing a final copy, without the labor of rewriting the whole paper several times. Language arts teachers are also capitalizing on the motivational aspects of the computer to help develop reading skills using CAL. For instance, programs have been written to give students practice in visual discrimination, vocabulary, synonyms and antonyms, and sentence comprehension. Most of these CAL programs contain pre-lesson and post-lesson exercises that measure skill development. While language arts teachers are quick to say that this skill building doesn't equate with reading, practice in these areas is necessary for improved reading.

Fine Arts

Teachers have found that instruction in music fundamentals can be enhanced with CAL. More specifically, the computer has combined sound and graphics to teach melody, harmony, rhythm, and instrumental methods. In art class, CAL has been successful in teaching basic art concepts. Computer programs have also been written to allow students to create their own art on the screen. In the area of dance instruction, the computer can use animation to teach students choreography. CAL is also used in the fine arts curriculum by entering into the computer the characteristics of works by prominent artists. Students can draw on this information to compare and contrast artists of different periods. The students can even create their own art by using the computer-generated analysis of works of art in a given period.

Special Education

Special education is another field in which advances in CAL are occurring at a rapid pace. Although it's impossible to acknowledge all the progress being made, several examples will illustrate the point. CAL has proven effective with deaf students because of the computer's ability to interact with the students through dialog. They are able to carry on a conversation with the computer without the barrier of their hearing loss. Certain physically handicapped students with little hand mobility have shown they can benefit from CAL lessons on computers when using specially designed paddles as input devices. The students can manipulate the paddles to create written language on the screen, a skill not attainable through conventional writing methods. As another example, students in learning disabilities classes have been successful in their experiences with CAL. Many students with learning problems benefit from the computer's ability to combine sound, graphics, pictorial information, and motion to teach a particular concept. They need these modes of learning in addition to the medium of print.

CAL has found a place in many curricular areas not mentioned above, such as business education, industrial arts, and foreign languages. However, the intent of this section is not to provide a comprehensive review of the literature of CAL in schools. Rather, the purpose is to convey the message that learning with computers is not restricted to a few isolated areas of the curriculum. CAL holds promise for our schools in ways we have just begun to understand.

HOW TO CHOOSE THE CAL
BEST SUITED TO YOUR STUDENTS

In deciding when and how to use the computer as an instructional helper in the classroom, you need to begin with the most basic question: How can the computer help in the teaching-learning process? Sometimes this question gets stated in an all-or-none way. In other words, the basic question becomes: Under what circumstances is the computer less expensive than other forms of teaching? With the question phrased in this manner, computers are put in direct competition with teachers, books, tutors, and so on. Some people argue that unless computer technology can demonstrate superiority over alternative ways of teaching, computers should not be used. In all fairness, though, we don't make the same demands of other teaching strategies. We don't insist that teachers only use books to teach a particular concept or solely use lectures to present a lesson. In effective classrooms, a range of teaching techniques is tried, in complementary fashion, to bring about learning. Similarly, then, we should expect computers to be used in conjunction with other methods, rather than in lieu of them, as we plan for instruction.

If you agree that computers can be helpful as a supplement to other teaching strategies, the question remains: How can it help? The answer depends on a complex set of factors such as: grade level, student ability level, subject area, objectives of the lesson, class size, and quality of available software on the topic. Since each teacher has to insert his or her own factors into the equation, the answers will vary, according to the individual. There is a common set of questions each teacher can ask, though, in deciding the most appropriate use of CAL:

- What is the purpose of my instruction (present new material, review material already taught, apply material learned to new situations)?
- What are my objectives for the lesson?
- What are the available CAL programs related to the lesson?

- Do any of these CAL programs complement my other teaching techniques?
- Would particular students benefit from the CAL programs?
- How can I incorporate the CAL programs into the classroom day?

Once you have responded to these questions, you are faced with evaluating the quality of the CAL programs that fit the lesson. To help assess the quality, you can apply the following checklist. Does the CAL program:

- Hold and maintain the interest of the student?
- Adequately explain what the lesson is about?
- Build on prior learning?
- Individualize material based on the student's interaction pattern?
- Allow the student to control the rate of presentation?
- Effectively use the machine capabilities of sound, color, and graphics?
- Give the student choices regarding the next sequence in the dialog, based on responses to the current sequence?

The purpose of Chapter 2 has been to give you a better understanding of how computers can serve as an aid to learning in the classroom. By applying the guidelines described in this chapter, you should be able to decide which CAL applications are best suited to your use. But the instructional capabilities of the computer aren't limited to CAL. Chapter 3 emphasizes how the computer can be used effectively to teach computer literacy.

CHAPTER 2 REFERENCES

Bork, Alfred, *Learning with Computers*, Bedford, MA: Digital Press, 1981.

Chambers, J., and J. Sprecher, "Computer Assisted Instruction: Current Trends and Critical Issues," *Communications of the ACM*, June 1980.

Dence, M., "Toward Defining the Role of CAI: A Review," *Educational Technology,* Nov. 1981.

Gagné , R. M., W. Wagner, and A. Rojas, "Planning and Authoring Computer-Assisted Instruction Lessons," *Educational Technology*, Sept. 1981.

Goles, Gordon, "Games as Teaching Tools: Effective Uses of the Child in All of Us," *Educational Computer*, Nov./Dec. 1982.

TEACHING AND LEARNING ABOUT COMPUTERS

Given the choice, not many of us would choose to be illiterate in any topic of socially declared value. Particularly, language illiteracy has been a major challenge of the schools for a long time. Amid some debate over whether or not today's students are less literate than their parents, educators continue to hold student literacy as a primary goal. But now a new debate is swiftly moving to center stage: Can we afford to graduate students who are computer illiterate? Actually, the debate isn't confined to the need for computer literacy; a companion issue screaming for resolution is: What is computer literacy? Within these issues lie several others. Are we really talking about literacy in the conventional sense? Do we need to create a new computer literacy curriculum? What are the major goals of a computer literacy curriculum? Can you have computer literacy for students without computer literate adults? Chapter 3 digs into these questions by taking a careful look at what students should be learning about computers.

50

CLARIFYING THE NEED
TO HAVE A COMPUTER LITERACY CURRICULUM

The rapid, almost meteoric surge of computer technology into education catches most teachers and administrators a little off guard. That is, we aren't prepared to answer the endless list of questions generated by having this new technology on our doorstep. One basic question we must face squarely is: Do we need to have a computer literacy curriculum? Undoubtedly, we are in an era being drastically affected by computer technology. Computers already have altered our lives in ways unimagined just several years ago. The projection for the future equally stretches our imagination. The only thing we can say for certain is that computer technology will continue to shape the lives of our school children as they assume our positions of leadership and responsibility.

With this sketchy projection as guide, what can we conclude about the need for a computer literacy curriculum in the schools? Given that we, as educators, shoulder the major responsibility for educating our nation's youth to effectively function in society, we also shoulder the responsibility for tailoring the curriculum accordingly. In the face of what we see unfolding in a world increasingly dependent on technology, we can safely conclude that the need exists to have students learn about computer technology. Beyond that, a mixture of emotion and experience leads educators to differing conclusions about what should make up a computer curriculum. The next section zooms in on the nub of the curriculum issue: the need for computer literacy.

UNSCRAMBLING THE CONFUSION
OVER COMPUTER LITERACY

Recently, a major midwestern paper carried the headline: "The Next National Disgrace: Why Johnny Can't Log On." At about the same time, a leading educational journal featured an article titled, "The Next Crisis in American Education: Computer Literacy." These banners typify the emotion aroused by a discussion on computer literacy. Keeping in mind the emotional component, you can imagine how quickly the debate heats up in the attempt to determine what's meant by the term "computer literacy." The heart of the debate centers on the meaning of "literacy."

In one camp reside those who claim that literacy means the ability to demonstrate certain skills required for the type of literacy in question. From this perspective, for example, language arts literacy means the ability to read and write language. Mathematics literacy requires the doing of mathematics. By analogy, computer literacy means the ability to compute, or to read and write computer language. Anything short of computing doesn't constitute literacy. For instance, however desirable it may be to know the parts of a computer or to recognize career opportunities open to those with computer training, mastery of these goals doesn't qualify someone for computer literacy.

Another camp harbors those who bristle at the thought of such a narrow definition. Proponents of a broader view of computer literacy maintain that literacy extends beyond doing; it represents the state of being informed, "cultured" and well versed. (A quick check of a dictionary confirms that both definitions are listed under "literacy.") To continue the argument advanced in the broad version, computer literacy includes the knowledge and skills students need to have about computers. Students can't be considered computer literate just because they can do programming. They need to develop certain values and understanding, along with skills, if they are to be truly computer literate.

As you can see, much of the emotion stirred by a discussion of computer literacy is more pointedly aroused over the term "literacy." As stated at the outset of this chapter, few of us would choose to be illiterate. We have been implicitly advised that literacy is a prerequisite to effectively functioning in our society. Therefore, common to each of our educational aspirations is the goal of individual literacy. As a society, we reinforce the value of such a goal. We chart literacy rates across countries. We trace the literacy pattern historically for the United States. In summary, our society clearly communicates the message that literacy is important.

When we enter into deliberations about computer literacy, we should do so fully aware of criticisms that may be leveled at our choice of terminology. First of all, literacy suggests a threshold condition, a spot on a continuum separating people into two dichotomous groups, the haves and the have-nots. You either are literate or you are not. Admittedly, one could argue that literacy is developmental; you could be almost literate, or almost illiterate. But as a society, we don't place much value on those of us who are almost literate. The literacy rates are given as the percentages of our population who have reached the threshold of literacy. In schools, we don't say 88 percent of our students passed the necessary tests to qualify as literate, while 7 percent almost passed. This 7 percent group is lumped into the same category as the others who are fully illiterate (as measured by performance on designated tests). So, unless carefully explained, literacy could convey a win-lose situation, being literate or illiterate, with nothing in between.

A second criticism for talking about computer literacy relates to our expectation of literacy in other subject areas. Typically, we refer to literacy in language arts and mathematics. Most of the graphs plotting literacy for our population use some form of reading, writing, and arithmetic as an index of the phenomenon measured. But we really don't apply the dichotomous term "literacy" to other basic skills areas. Of course we could, and maybe, on occasion do, refer to skills such as social studies literacy, science literacy, and interpersonal relationships literacy. Usually, though, a discussion of basic skills centers on the developmental nature of these subjects. Emphasis is placed on moving students along a continuum of learning, taking them as far as their respective abilities permit during their public schooling.

So the confusion over what constitutes computer literacy really boils down to a difference in interpretation about what literacy means. The camp claiming the more narrow definition, the camp holding out for an expanded definition, and the camp arguing to drop the label "literacy," may not really differ over what's important for students to learn about computers.

PROPOSED AIM OF
A COMPUTER LITERACY CURRICULUM

What, then, *is* important for students to learn regarding computers? Based on our country's beliefs about what is important in other basic skill areas, and consistent with most of the program development work in the area of computers, the following general goal emerges as central to a computer curriculum: Each student should develop those skills, attitudes and knowledge about computer technology necessary to function effectively in our technological world of today and tomorrow.

Endorsement of this goal concomitantly endorses several other beliefs. First, a computer curriculum should devote balanced attention to the domains of knowing, doing, and feeling. Without prescribing a universal balance to fit all schools and classrooms, it is important for students to learn about computer technology and apply these concepts in the form of interacting with computers, while developing positive attitudes about computer technology and its impact on the individual and society. A second belief is that these skills are necessary to function effectively in our society. A quick snapshot of a typical day reveals how we constantly interact with computer technology in ways not conceived even a short time ago. Finally, the general goal stated above contains a belief that the identified dimensions of a computer curriculum must be future oriented. We simply can't build programs on the assumption that the world as we now know it will be the same when our children experience it decades later. We must be futuristic in our thinking. We need to anticipate what tomorrow's world of technology may look like, and develop programs to prepare students accordingly.

FOUR PROGRAM GOALS OF
A COMPUTER LITERACY CURRICULUM

Even though the general goal stated above implies several beliefs about what a computer curriculum should look like, it doesn't provide specific direction. To help point some direction, four program goals are outlined below. These goals represent a synthesis of current theory and practice regarding computer technology in the curriculum.

Goal 1: Students should understand how computer technology works.

A discussion of this goal must begin with a caveat: Computer technology is changing faster than a person's ability to learn it. On the surface, then, it may seem pointless to try making sense of how a computer works when it may not work that way in the near future. But, a conceptual understanding of today's technology makes the transition easier when trying to understand future technology. As an illustration, suppose you were involved in computer work when the machines consisted of huge vacuum tubes and filled the equivalent of your school building. An understanding of these dinosaurs of the recent past would make it much easier to grasp how contemporary computers operate.

Specific objectives for this program goal can be as detailed or general as you decide. Sample objectives include the following:

- Describe how each generation of computers has evolved.
- Define basic computer terms.
- Identify major components of a computer.
- Differentiate among micro, mini, and mainframe computers.
- Describe how computers process information.

Goal 2: Students should understand the capabilities and limitations of computer technology in our society.

A recent survey of students in computer classes at the secondary level revealed that they understood how computer technology works, but that they lacked a clear understanding of what computers can and cannot do. As teachers and administrators responsible for a computer literacy curriculum, we have a major responsibility to insure that students don't develop false impressions about the capabilities and limitations of computers. It's tempting for students to assign some sort of omniscient power to computers. It becomes incumbent, therefore, upon teachers to dispel the myths about computers and expose the many limitations inherent in this machinery. At the other extreme, we are charged with the task of making sure students respect the enormous capabilities packed into a computer. With an adequate understanding of what computers can do well, students are more likely to use the technology to its full potential. Some objectives within this goal are to:

- Explain how computer technology affects our daily lives.
- Describe applications for which computers are best suited.
- Describe applications for which computers aren't suited.

- Identify career fields related to computers.
- Identify ethical principles in the use of computer technology.
- Identify potential harmful effects of the inappropriate use of computers.
- Describe factors that limit computer applications.
- Distinguish between human and computer capabilities.

Goal 3: Students should be able to operate and program a computer to answer a variety of personal, academic, and professional needs.

Because the field of computer technology in schools is so new, very little guidance exists as educators struggle to determine what a computer literacy curriculum should look like. An area that does have a proven track record is the field of computer programming. Many universities have well-established Computer Science departments that specialize in teaching programming and related topics. Consequently, a lot of schools turned to computer programming courses in response to the cry for computer literacy. Early curriculum development efforts in computer technology treated a course in BASIC programming as synonymous with computer literacy.

Even now, programming is the cornerstone of a typical computer literacy curriculum. The rationale for this is straightforward. In order to understand how a computer processes information, you need the ability to tell the computer how to do the processing. One of the quickest ways to demystify computers is to master the skills necessary to control their operation. This mastery over the computer also leads to a feeling of confidence in using this new technology, an extremely desirable objective in its own right.

Reasons for learning to program extend beyond fulfilling class requirements. Ideally, students will transfer these skills into non-academic areas. For instance, numerous anecdotes in journals and the popular press document how enterprising individuals have used their programming skills to create second businesses. In fact, many people are working part time out of their homes in what has been labeled the "mushrooming electronic cottage industry." Other personal accounts confirm the variety of personal uses people find for their programming skills, such as computerized records for the softball team, money management systems, and mailing lists for sending greeting cards to friends and relatives. These examples barely scratch the surface of creative ways to activate programming skills first learned in a computer literacy curriculum.

Clearly, the skill of operating and programming a computer will remain a major component in the typical computer curriculum. Perhaps the course content will change as more powerful programming languages emerge and more sophisticated ways evolve for using the computer. However, with one eye toward flexibility in the curriculum, we can expect to see the following sample objectives under Goal 3:

- Use a prepared program in a computer.
- Create a simple program.
- Draw a flowchart to order steps in solving a problem.
- Feel confident in the ability to use a computer.
- Describe experiences with computers in a positive way.
- Develop more sophisticated programming skills as demanded by your particular needs.

Goal 4: Students should be able to use computer applications to answer a variety of personal, academic, and professional needs.

Not everyone will grow up to be a computer programmer. More specifically, not everyone will exit the computer literacy curriculum with the programming skills necessary for some of the applications described above. Foremost, though, is the expectation that everyone will grow up applying prepared computer programs in ways that satisfy a variety of needs. As we witness the widespread proliferation of computers in classroom, office and home, we will also witness major advances in the quantity and quality of computer software. To a large extent, these new programs will respond to our personal and professional needs. Already, we can take advantage of programs that compute our taxes, control our home utilities, monitor home alarm systems, and connect us with nationwide listings of homes for sale, just to name a tiny fraction of personal applications. Of course, computer power in the office is heavily used and will grow more sophisticated as we continue to stretch the frontier of computer technology. The point of this discussion, however, is not to convince you that the computer has a myriad of applications ready and waiting. The point is to emphasize the importance of students learning to apply computer power to meet their needs. Teachers can't provide students with canned applications that have universal utility. They *can* teach students the "how"—how to use computers to their advantage—now and in the future.

To achieve this goal, the computer curriculum should provide a range of experiences so students have a broad perspective on computer applications. Here are sample objectives for Goal 4:

- Spend ample leisure time using a computer.
- Use computer technology to efficiently handle home management tasks.
- Access a variety of news, stock report, and library services via computer.
- Apply problem-solving capabilities of the computer in academic work.
- Use computer technology as a database manager in professional situations.

RESOLVING CRITICAL ISSUES BEFORE DECIDING ON A COMPUTER LITERACY CURRICULUM

However tempting it may be to embrace the preceding goals so you can get on with planning and implementation, several important questions must first be addressed. You may find that your responses have a major effect on shaping your next step, ranging from a decision against teaching computer literacy to the conclusion that all children at all grade levels should receive some instruction toward computer literacy. The following is a core set of questions for your consideration. Local circumstances will dictate others.

What Is Meant by Computer Literacy?

Returning to the argument posed earlier in the chapter, teachers and administrators have to get beyond slogans before they can effectively discuss curriculum issues. In your school environment, is literacy synonymous with computer programming, or does the term include knowledge about computers as well? When the community, the press, staff members and school district decision-makers begin deliberations about the importance of computer literacy, it's critical that they focus on a common understanding of the label (if the label is used). The tendency sometimes is to dismiss disagreements at this level as a difference in semantics, obstructing progress toward the real goal. A collection of bumps and bruises, however, serves as a reminder that often these differences aren't just semantic; if they aren't resolved in the critical stages of discussion, they can rear their ugly heads at a point when it's difficult to iron them out.

Do Teachers See a Need for Computer Literacy?

The history of innovations in schools is replete with attempts at change coming to a final rest *outside* schoolhouse and classroom doors. Unless teachers see a need for teaching computer literacy, all of the fanfare and top-down edicts a district can muster won't assure successful implementation. Because virtually all teachers want what's best for their students, they can offer a realistic perspective regarding whether and where computer literacy belongs in their curriculum. Maintaining teacher perspectives is equally important through participation in the planning and implementation of a computer literacy project.

How Do You Add a New Curriculum Without Creating Curriculum Overload?

Apart from the positive aspects of offering a computer literacy curriculum, you need to squarely face the issue of adding something else to an already packed curriculum. Few districts could claim that there is plenty of room in the school day for something else to teach. In most cases, the opposite condition exists. Teachers find it difficult to squeeze into the current curriculum everything they have agreed to cover during the year. To come knocking at the classroom door with yet another curriculum area is to invite added frustration bordering on panic. So you should weigh the question carefully and arrive at a rational response that considers all the other curriculum demands along with this new push for a computer curriculum. In the final analysis, if you decide to go ahead with such a program, at least you can strongly justify to teachers why the decision was made to commence with planning.

What Is the District's Commitment to Planning and Implementation?

Even though this question could be asked of each possible computer application, it's particularly significant in the area of a computer literacy curriculum. It's difficult enough to get additional district resources earmarked for a special project. It's doubly difficult to get the necessary commitment for a multi-year planning and implementation effort affecting many, if not all, grade levels. Even if the commitment is made, you are faced with the possibility of change in personnel, along with an accompanying change in priorities. Perhaps the single most important question demanding a positive answer is: Will adequate resources be available to carry out the project? Otherwise, you face the very real danger that your carefully conceived computer literacy curriculum will assume a spot alongside other lifeless projects in the innovation graveyard if long-range commitment of financial resources is not made.

These questions aren't meant as obstacles to needlessly impede a worthwhile project. They are meant to help clear the way, and to remove obstacles about issues that, once resolved, make for smoother planning and implementation.

TWO EXEMPLARY MODELS OF A COMPUTER CURRICULUM

Judging by recent accounts in journals, newsletters, and the popular press, successful computer curriculums are sprouting in districts across the nation. While similarities exist in these programs, it's naive to expect a universal standard to emerge as the "one best model." It would be equally naive, though, to discount the depth and breadth of experience some districts bring to the field of computer technology. Specifically, two pioneers in the field are the Cupertino Union School District and the Minnesota Educational Computing Consortium (MECC). This section features recent curriculum development work by these two leaders in the field.

Cupertino Computer Literacy Curriculum

Much of the innovative work in computer technology comes from an area dubbed the Silicon Valley, nestled in the heartland of California. One of the most active districts in the valley has been the Cupertino School District, a K-8 district of about 13,000 students.

After some initial exploration with computers beginning in 1977, the school board decided, in 1981, to allocate capital funds for widespread piloting of the computer curriculum during the 1981-82 school year, with an eye toward full-scale implementation in 1982-83.

Under the Cupertino Plan, the use of microcomputers is a part of regular classroom activities in grades 3-6. In grades 7-8, students may take a course in Computer Awareness and Introductory Programming. The major objectives of the Cupertino Union School District Computer Curriculum are outlined in Figure 3-1.

In reflecting on Cupertino's experience in computer curriculum development, District Computer Resource Specialist Bobby Goodson offers this advice (*The Computing Teacher*, 1981, p. 27):

"The success of a program like this, introduced throughout a district, is dependent upon a well-developed in-service program, with wide participation that gives teachers a good foundation to build on. We have reached this point because we have taken time (over three years) and worked in stages. I think a district would have difficulty instituting such a program as a complete package. People need to be trained and ready with an explicit curriculum in hand if the program is to be truly successful."

Based on progress to date, the Cupertino School District has certainly heeded Goodson's advice.

FIGURE 3-1. CUPERTINO UNION SCHOOL DISTRICT COMPUTER CURRICULUM OBJECTIVES*

THE STUDENT WILL:

A. Develop a vocabulary of common computer terms.

	K-3	4-6	7-8
Define (and spell) basic computer terms.	I	R	R
Differentiate between analog and digital devices.			I
Tell what a computer is and how it works.	I	R	R
Differentiate among computers, calculators, and electronic games.		I	R
Differentiate among micro-, mini-, and mainframe computers, and identify the five major components of any computer.		I	R
Define "software" and "hardware," and list two examples of each.		I	R
Define "input" and "output," and give an example of each.		I	R
Define the term "data base."			I

B. Be familiar with the history of computing devices and the development of computers.

	K-3	4-6	7-8
Describe the historical development of computing devices.		I	R

Note: Symbols indicate the level at which objectives and activities are introduced (I) and reviewed or reinforced (R).

*Source: "Cupertino School District Develops Computer Literacy Curriculum," *The Computing Teacher,* 9-81, pp. 31-34.

	K-3	4-6	7-8
Describe the historical development of computing devices as related to other scientific devices.		I	R
Tell about a person or an event that influenced the historical development of computing devices.		I	R
Tell about the history of Silicon Valley.			I
List of the characteristics of each generation of computers.		I	R

C. Develop an understanding of how computers are used.

	K-3	4-6	7-8
Explain ways computers affect our lives.		I	R
List several ways that computers are used in everyday life.	I	R	R
Identify ways that computers are used to help consumers.		I	R
Describe how computer simulations are used in problem-solving.		I	R
Identify ways in which computers help make decisions.			I
Explain how computers are used in predicting, interpreting, and evaluating data.			I
Explain how computer models are used in testing and evaluating hypotheses.			I
List several ways computers are used to process statistical data.			I
List several sampling techniques and statistical methods used in the social sciences.			I
Explain the meaning of "word processing."			I
Describe the computer's place in our growing understanding of science.			I
Illustrate the importance of the computer in modern science and industry.		I	R

	K-3	4-6	7-8
Explain how computer graphics are used in engineering, science, art, etc.			I
Explain how computers are used as devices for gathering and processing data.			I
Describe computer applications such as those consisting of information storage and retrieval, process control, aids to decision making, computation and data processing, simulation, and modeling.			I
Show that computers are best suited to tasks that require speed, accuracy, and repeated operations.			I
Describe situations that limit computer use (cost, availability of software and storage capacity).			I
Describe some advantages and disadvantages of a data base of personal information.			I
Describe problems related to the "invasion of privacy."			I
Describe ways in which computers are used to commit a wide variety of crimes and how these crimes are detected.			I

D. Learn about computer-related career opportunities.

	K-3	4-6	7-8
Identify career fields related to computer development and use.		I	R
State the value of computer skills for future employment.			I
Describe how computers are used by sociologists and other social scientists.			I
Describe some of the ways computers are used in the information and language-related careers.			I
Show how a scientist would use a computer.			I

	K-3	4-6	7-8

E. Gain a nontechnical understanding of how computers function.

	K-3	4-6	7-8
Explain that a computer design is based on standard logic patterns.			I
Explain the basic operation of a computer system in terms of the input of data or information, the processing of data or information, and the output of data or information.			I
Describe the techniques computers use to process data such as searching, sorting, deleting, updating, summarizing, moving.			I
Recognize the need for data to be organized to be useful.			I
Explain the statement: "Computer mistakes" are mistakes made by people.			I
Identify common tasks that are NOT suited to computer solution.	I	R	R
Define "computer program."		I	R
Recognize the relationship of a program, or input, to the result, or output.		I	R
Evaluate whether output is reasonable in terms of the problem to be solved and the given input.		I	R
State what will happen if instructions are not properly stated in the precise language for that computer.		I	R
List at least three computer languages and identify the purposes for which each is used.			I
State that BASIC is one of the languages used most commonly by microcomputers.		I	R
Explain the existence of several variations in BASIC.		I	R

	K-3	4-6	7-8
F. Learn to use a computer.			
Become familiar with a microcomputer through its use in the classroom.	I	R	R
Use a prepared program in a microcomputer.		I	R
State the meaning of "algorithm."			I
Explain what is being accomplished by a given algorithm.			I
Follow and give correct output for a given algorithm.			I
Describe the standard flow-chart symbols.		I	R
Read and explain a flow chart.		I	R
Draw a flow chart to represent a solution to a proposed problem.		I	R
Order specific steps in the solution of a problem.		I	R
List several fundamental BASIC statements and commands.		I	R
Differentiate between random computer commands and computer programs.		I	R
State the difference between system commands and program statements.			I
Create a simple program in BASIC.		I	R
Use the computer to accomplish a mathematical task.		I	R
Translate mathematical relations and functions into a computer program.			I
Use a computer as a word processor.			I

MECC Framework for Developing a Computer Literacy Curriculum

The Minnesota Educational Computing Consortium has been a leader for years in promoting the use of computers in schools. A major project undertaken by MECC and funded by the National

Science Foundation is entitled "Assessing Computer Literacy" (grant number SED 79-20087). This research effort produced the computer literacy objectives shown in Figure 3-2. These objectives, organized into six categories or domains, are numbered with two values. The first one designates the objectives as elementary ("1") or advanced ("2"), and the second value is a sequence number. Since there are limitations on the amount of material that can be covered in a curriculum, the project directors have designated certain objectives (identified with an asterisk) as core objectives. According to the directors (Anderson, Klassen, Krohn, Smith-Cunnien, 1982), these core objectives probably could be achieved within a one-year secondary course.

FIGURE 3-2. MINNESOTA EDUCATIONAL COMPUTING CONSORTIUM (MECC) COMPUTER LITERACY OBJECTIVES*

1. HARDWARE (H)

Objective

*H.1.1   *Identify* the five major components of a computer: input equipment, memory unit, control unit, arithmetic unit, output equipment.

*H.1.2   *Identify* the basic operation of a computer *system*. Input of data or information, processing of data or information, output of data or information.

*H.1.3   *Distinguish* between hardware and software.

*H.1.4   *Identify* how a person can access a computer; e.g.,
　　　　1. via a keyboard terminal
　　　　　　a. at computer site
　　　　　　b. at any distance via telephone lines
　　　　2. via punched or marked cards
　　　　3. via other magnetic media (tape, diskette)

*H.1.5   *Recognize* the rapid growth of computer hardware since the 1940s.

*H.2.1 *Determine* that the basic components function as an *interconnected system* under the control of a *stored program* developed *by a person.*

*H.2.2 *Compare* computer processing and storage capabilities to the human brain, listing some general similarities and differences.

2. SOFTWARE AND DATA PROCESSING (S)

Objective

S.1.1 *Identify* the fact that we communicate with computers through a binary code.

S.1.2 *Identify* the need for data to be organized if they are to be useful.

S.1.3 *Identify* the fact that information is data that have been given meaning.

S.1.4 *Identify* the fact that data are coded mechanisms for communication.

S.1.5 *Identify* the fact that communication is the transmission of information via coded messages.

*S.1.6 *Identify* the fact that data processing involves the transformation of data by means of a set of predefined rules.

*S.1.7 *Recognize* that a computer needs instructions to operate.

*S.1.8 *Recognize* that a computer gets instructions from a program written in a programming language.

*S.1.9 *Recognize* that a computer is capable of storing a program and data.

*S.1.10 *Recognize* that computers process data by searching, sorting, deleting, updating, summarizing, moving, etc.

*S.2.1   *Select* an appropriate attribute for the ordering of data for a particular task.

S.2.2   *Design* an elementary data structure for a given application (that is, provide order for the data).

S.2.3   *Design* an elementary coding system for a given application.

3. APPLICATIONS (A)

Objective

*A.1.1   *Recognize* specific uses of computers in some of the following fields:
   a. medicine
   b. law enforcement
   c. education
   d. engineering
   e. business
   f. transportation
   g. military defense systems
   h. weather prediction
   i. recreation
   j. government
   k. libraries
   l. creative arts

A.1.2   *Identify* the fact that there are many programming languages suitable for a particular application in business or science.

*A.1.3   *Recognize* that the following activities are among the major types of applications of the computer:
   a. information storage and retrieval
   b. simulation and modeling
   c. process control, decision-making
   d. computation
   e. data processing

*A.1.4   *Recognize* that computers are generally good at information-processing tasks that benefit from:
  a. speed
  b. accuracy
  c. repetitiveness

*A.1.5   *Recognize* that some limiting considerations for using computers are:
  a. cost
  b. software availability
  c. storage capacity

*A.1.6   *Recognize* the basic features of a computerized information system.

*A.2.1   *Determine* how computers can assist the consumer.

*A.2.2   *Determine* how computers can assist in a decision-making process.

A.2.3   *Assess* the feasibility of potential applications.

A.2.4   *Develop* a new application.

4. IMPACT (I)

Objective

*I.1.1   *Distinguish* among the following careers:
  a. keypuncher/key operator
  b. computer operator
  c. computer programmer
  d. systems analyst
  e. computer scientist

*I.1.2   *Recognize* that computers are used to commit a wide variety of serious crimes but especially stealing money and information.

*I.1.3   *Recognize* that identification codes (numbers) and passwords are a primary means for restricting use of computer systems, computer programs, and data files.

I.1.4   *Recognize* that procedures for detecting computer-based crimes are not well developed.

*I.1.5   *Identify* some advantages or disadvantages of a data base containing personal information on a large number of people (e.g., the list might include value for research and potential for privacy invasion).

I.1.6   *Recognize* several regulatory procedures (e.g., privilege to review one's own file and restrictions on use of universal personal identifiers), which help to insure the integrity of personal data files.

*I.1.7   *Recognize* that most "privacy problems" are characteristic of large information files, whether or not they are computerized.

*I.1.8   *Recognize* that computerization both increases and decreases employment.

*I.1.9   *Recognize* that computerization both personalizes and impersonalizes procedures in such fields as education.

*I.1.10 *Recognize* that computerization can lead to both great independence and dependence upon one's tools.

*I.1.11 *Recognize* that, while computers do not have the mental capacity that humans do, through techniques such as artificial intelligence, computers have been able to modify their own instruction set and do many of the same information-processing tasks as humans.

*I.1.12 *Recognize* that alleged "computer mistakes" are usually mistakes made by people.

*I.2.1   *Plan* a strategy for tracing and correcting a computer-related error such as a billing error.

I.2.2   *Explain* how computers make public surveillance more feasible.

*I.2.3   *Recognize* that even though a person does not go near a computer, he or she is affected indirectly because the society has changed in many sectors as a consequence of computerization.

I.2.4   *Explain* how computers can be used to have an impact on the distribution and use of economic and political power.

5. PROGRAMMING AND ALGORITHMS (P)

Objective

P.1.1   *Recognize* the definition of "algorithm."

*P.1.2   *Follow* and give the correct output for a simple algorithm.

*P.1.3   Given a simple algorithm, *explain* what it accomplishes (i.e., interpret and generalize).

*P.2.1   *Modify* a simple algorithm to accomplish a new but related task.

P.2.2   *Detect* logic errors in an algorithm.

P.2.3   *Correct* errors in an improperly functioning algorithm.

P.2.4   *Develop* an algorithm for solving a specific problem.

P.2.5   *Develop* an algorithm that can be used to solve a set of similar problems.

6. VALUES (V)

Objective

*V.1   *Do not feel* fear, anxiety, or intimidation from computer experiences.

*V.2   *Feel* confident about one's ability to use and control computers.

*V.3   *Value* efficient information processing, provided that it does not neglect accuracy, the protection of individual rights, and social needs.

*V.4   *Value* computerization of routine tasks, so long as it frees people to engage in other activities and is not done as an end in itself.

*V.5   *Value* increased communication and availability of information made possible through computer use, provided that it does not violate personal rights to privacy and accuracy of personal data.

V.6   *Value* economic benefits of computerization for a society.

V.7   *Enjoy and desire* work or play with computers, especially computer-assisted learning.

V.8   *Describe* past experiences with computers in positive-affect words (e.g., fun, exciting, challenging, etc.).

V.9   Given an opportunity, *spend* some free time using a computer.

Note: '*' indicates core objectives.

---

*Source: Anderson, R., D. Klassen, K. Krohn, and P. Smith-Cunnien, "Assessing Computer Literacy," St. Paul, MN: Minnesota Educational Computing Consortium, Final Report, 1982.

Taken separately, each computer literacy curriculum just described may have minimal influence on a computer curriculum project you undertake. Taken in context with the other issues discussed in this chapter, these models lead to provocative discussions about what a computer literacy curriculum should look like.

But before launching a large-scale computer literacy curriculum project, you should carefully consider another force competing for the use of computers, namely the noninstructional applications of computers. Chapter 4 examines the power of the computer as a management assistant to the teacher.

CHAPTER 3 REFERENCES

Anderson, C., "Teaching Computer Literacy: Guidelines for a Six Week Course," *Electronic Learning*, Nov. 1981.

Anderson, R. E., D. L. Klassen, and D. C. Johnson, "In Defense of a Comprehensive View of Computer Literacy—A Reply to Luehrmann," *Mathematics Teacher*, Dec. 1981.

Anderson, R., and D. L. Klassen, "A Conceptual Framework for Developing Computer Literacy Instruction," *AEDS Journal*, Spring 1981.

Anderson, R., D. L. Klassen, K. Krohn, and P. Smith-Cunnien, *Assessing Computer Literacy*, St. Paul, MN: Minnesota Educational Computing Consortium, Final Report, 1982.

Bitter, G., "The Road to Computer Literacy: A Scope and Sequence Model," *Electronic Learning*, Sept. 1982.

Course Goals in Computer Education, K-12, Portland, OR: Northwest Regional Laboratory, 1979.

"Cupertino School District Develops Computer Literacy Curriculum," *The Computing Teacher*, Sept. 1981.

Greene, M., "Literacy for What?" *Phi Delta Kappan*, Jan. 1982.

Johnson, D. C., R. E. Anderson, T. P. Hansen, and D. L. Klassen, "Computer Literacy—What Is It?" *Mathematics Teacher*, Feb. 1980.

Luehrmann, A., "Computer Literacy—What Should It Be?" *Mathematics Teacher*, Dec. 1981.

Molnar, A., "The Coming of Computer Literacy: Are We Prepared for It?" *Educational Technology*, Jan. 1981.

Watt, D., "Computer Literacy: What Should Schools Do About It?" *Instructor*, Oct. 1981.

4

FREEING TEACHERS ═══ OF TEDIOUS TASKS: COMPUTER MANAGED INSTRUCTION

As teachers and administrators, we know from experience that the school day gets carved into little pieces as cultural arts programs, announcements, tornado drills, and Halloween parties compete for students' time in school. Even when there are no "interruptions" in learning, classroom teachers find that the amount of time devoted to instruction is reduced proportionately to the amount of time required to manage the instructional process. This intrusion into precious instructional time is evidenced by the reports, forms, and more forms demanded of teachers. Teacher frustration over this paper blizzard is heightened by the realization that the number of minutes in a school day is finite. It can't be expanded or reduced at will. Whenever someone or something takes up a chunk of time, your instructional time is diminished. One response to this predicament is to discover ways to more efficiently manage the time available. Not surprisingly, many teachers and administrators are finding that computer technology offers a sensible solution to the problem of mushrooming management demands on the teacher, coupled with a steady decline in actual teaching time. The purpose of this chapter is to pinpoint how the technology of computer managed instruction (CMI) can put more of the "teach" back in teaching, by letting the computer do more of the managing.

ASSUMPTIONS UNDERLYING CMI

Before you can seriously consider implementing computer managed instruction (CMI), you need a clear picture of just what the concept entails. The image of wheeling a microcomputer into any classroom and assigning it the management tasks not chosen by the teacher is a misrepresentation of CMI. Specifically, computer managed instruction rests on a framework supported by three interconnected assumptions. These points, adapted from the conceptualization first proposed by Baker (1978), are described below.

Mastery Learning

The idea of mastery learning has been around in various forms for the last twenty years. Basically, mastery learning proponents argue that nearly all children can learn if they are provided the same opportunity and quality of instruction. The difference in learning patterns, then, lies in the time required to understand the material.

In theory, mastery learning assumes several things. First, a curriculum must be divided into smaller units, each able to be broken down into measurable student objectives. Second, student progress on these objectives must be able to be gauged by performance, usually on a quiz or test. Subsequent teaching depends on how students perform on the tests scattered throughout the instructional units. Third, given appropriate teaching and adequate time, virtually all students can master the curriculum. Time becomes the index of ability: children of varying abilities can all learn the material if the teacher allows for individuals to be flexibile in the amount of time they spend on the material. A fourth and final assumption is that mastery learning does not imply equal learning. Even though 90 percent of the students master a particular objective, many extend their learning far beyond the mastery level. In other words, mastery learning theory doesn't put a ceiling on what students can accomplish. It only dictates a minimum so they can't drop below an acceptable level of learning.

In practice, mastery learning tends to follow a predictable scenario. The teacher identifies what is important for students to learn, decides the acceptable level of learning, selects the appropriate objectives given data on prior performance, tests students on the lesson currently taught, and makes subsequent assignments based on evaluation of current performance.

Although the sequence sounds fairly rigid, the concept of mastery learning can accommodate a range of teaching styles. For instance, two teachers in the same grade, at the same school, could employ mastery learning techniques without compromising their individual teaching beliefs. The common theme woven into mastery learning is that the teacher knows what is important to teach, identifies an acceptable level of student performance, and teaches (even reteaches) until student performance reaches the mastery level.

Individualization

The concept of individualized instruction can be described in many different ways. For our purposes, we will confine such a description to assumptions about the student as learner.

The primary focus of any individualized instructional program is the growth of the individual learner. Because children differ according to their interests, emotional needs, rates of learning, styles of learning, and academic as well as nonschool experiences, advocates of individualized instruction claim students should:

- have the opportunity to learn at their own individual rates
- progress in their learning without needlessly omitting or repeating any part of the curriculum

- receive instruction commensurate with their learning style
- receive instruction geared to their interests
- progress through the curriculum according to goals tailored to fit the individual student's needs

By taking these beliefs about the learner and translating them into curriculum considerations, you end up with an individualized instructional program that:

- provides different goals within a curriculum based on individual differences
- offers alternative paths for moving through the individually tailored curriculum
- incorporates varying instructional methods according to individual needs
- accommodates varying rates of progress within a curriculum

Obviously, not every individualized program encompasses all of these characteristics. In fact, very few do. Most individualized instruction varies the rate of progress through a common curriculum for all students. Even with this narrow interpretation of the concept, many teachers and administrators argue that children learning at their own pace is justification enough for calling their program an individualized one.

Teacher as Manager of Instruction

The dominant image of the classroom teacher is a person working energetically to help students learn. Hardly anyone gives much thought to the role of teacher as manager—that is, anyone but teachers and administrators. Yet a lot of evidence exists to show that the teacher spends a considerable amount of time managing during the school day. Specifically, the teacher is charged with the responsibility of managing student behavior and the information needed to make instructional decisions. This section focuses on the latter role, the teacher as manager of instruction.

Some of the information to be managed consists of seemingly endless reports required by the "central office." The information most directly affecting students consists of the formal and informal data you use in your instructional decision-making. The issue is not whether you should be a manager; you are and you will continue to be. The issue is what information you choose or are required to manage. For example, given time as a scarce resource, you could spend it:

- developing tests
- administering tests
- scoring tests
- recording scores
- keeping track of student progress
- analyzing data to decide on the most appropriate grouping patterns for instruction
- using information to diagnose the needs of each student
- prescribing the next instructional activity for a student, based on accumulated information on his or her performance
- examining group performance to assess teaching effectiveness
- analyzing group performance as one means of curriculum evaluation
- completing periodic student grade reports

The list of potential management tasks could go on indefinitely. The point, however, is not the scope of these duties, but rather the need for you to decide how to allocate your time among competing management demands. A major assumption of computer managed instruction is that routine, tedious classroom tasks can be managed by the computer, freeing you to manage information you are most trained for: diagnosing performance data and prescribing appropriate instruction based on those data. This role reflects a philosophic dimension to CMI easily obscured by the emphasis on managing data. Teachers use information in some fashion to make instructional decisions, but many teachers spend so much time scoring, evaluating, and reporting that they have little time for making decisions about the educational welfare of the students. CMI proponents argue loudly that your managerial responsibilities should be concentrated in the area of instructional decision-making related to identified educational goals, not in charting productivity.

The three assumptions underlying Computer Managed Instruction are not discrete, unrelated entities. Admittedly, an instructional framework could include some of the themes described above without including the others. In fact, the three themes could exist side by side without the presence of computer technology. But combining the concepts of mastery learning, individualization, and teacher as instructional manager yields a sound philosophical position about how instruction should be managed in the classroom.

IMPROVING INSTRUCTIONAL MANAGEMENT WITH COMPUTER POWER

Weaving the power of the computer into these themes produces an even stronger position, because the computer can assert its superiority in speed and accuracy of collecting, storing, analyzing, and reporting data, leaving you free to assert your superiority in the management of instructional decisions.

The computer's contribution to a CMI system is limited primarily by the computer capability and the design of the CMI computer program. For example, most CMI systems require at least 48K (48,000 characters) of memory and one or two disk drives. Even with this much power, the computer can't handle your needs if the program isn't designed to accommodate your specific CMI requirements. Assuming, though, you have ample computer memory and an adequate computer program to handle your CMI needs, the technology exists to produce just about any kind of data request you can make. The information provided by a CMI system can be roughly classified as fixed and variable. Fixed data, in other words, are data entered into the computer that remain unchanged during a school year, unless changes occur in classroom conditions. Examples of fixed data are teacher name, student names, course title, units of instruction, and unit objectives. Variable data include student performance scores, instructional time periods, and instructional grouping patterns. To get a better picture of how this information is used in a CMI system, let's look at the most common reports produced in computer managed instruction. We will examine the hypothetical reports of Mrs. Albert's fifth-grade math class. Mrs. Albert relies on the CMI system to relieve her of the following tedious tasks.

Monitoring Individual Student Progress

For a curriculum based on mastery learning and individualized instruction, close monitoring of each individual's progress becomes a necessity, not just a luxury. If Mrs. Albert wants to know how Antonio is progressing on Topics 34-38, she requests a Student Progress Report. From this report, shown in Figure 4-1, Mrs. Albert can tell how Antonio is performing across topics, determine which objectives are causing him particular difficulty, and note the time frame he has followed in studying the objectives contained in this report.

FIGURE 4-1. NEW MATH PROGRAM

		Assessment
STUDENT PROGRESS REPORT		
WINSLOW SCHOOL		
TEACHER: MRS. ALBERT		
STUDENT: ANTONIO PEREZ	Performance	Date
DATE : 11/18/83		
TOPIC 34: UNITS OF WEIGHT		
OBJECTIVES 1. Compares measurements of weights of two objects	M	10/26/83
2. Orders weights of three objects	M	10/26/83

TOPIC 35: ANGLES AND SYMMETRY

OBJECTIVES 1. Identifies the line of symmetry for given figures   M   11/1/83

2. Compares two angles to determine which is larger   P   11/2/83

3. Identifies a right angle among several figures   P   11/2/83

TOPIC 36: NUMBERS 0-999

OBJECTIVES 1. Reads numbers from 0-999   M   11/8/83

2. Physically or pictorially represents numbers 0-999   M   11/9/83

TOPIC 37: ADDITION AND SUBTRACTION PROBLEMS 0-999

OBJECTIVES 1. Computes sum 0-999   P   11/16/83

2. Computes difference 0-999   P   11/16/83

TOPIC 38: MEASURING LENGTH

OBJECTIVES 1. Accurately measures length of given object   X   11/16/83

2. Compares lengths of two objects   X   11/16/83

<u>Note</u>
M = Mastery
P = Progress
X = Not Introduced

Monitoring Group Progress

Mrs. Albert can also request a report showing how her entire class did on these topics. As illustrated in Figure 4-2, the Group Progress Report resembles a teacher's gradebook, listing students alphabetically along with their "grades" on each objective within a topic. Mrs. Albert might conclude from this report that the class is having difficulty with adding and subtracting problems, 0-999. The teacher may choose to use alternative strategies for teaching this topic, and then request another Group Progress Report to see how the class progressed from the initial time period.

Grouping Students for Instruction

At the heart of any individualized instructional program is the idea of variably pacing students through the curriculum. Mrs. Albert agrees with this assumption, and tries to tailor her instruction to the rate of learning exhibited by each student. The computer component of her CMI system helps her by providing the report outlined in Figure 4-3. As students master objectives and are ready to move on, Mrs. Albert requests a grouping report. In this example, the teacher wants to know which students have satisfactorily completed Topics 35 and 36. These students will be assigned the next topic for study. The grouping recommendation report proves particularly useful when teachers group students across homerooms for instructional purposes.

Diagnosing and Prescribing Instruction

Virtually all CMI systems rely on diagnosis and prescription as a cornerstone of the curriculum. Mrs. Albert firmly believes that instructional decisions should be based on a diagnosis of previous performance and a prescription for what to do next. The report shown in Figure 4-4 helps her with this decision-making. The system operating at Mrs. Albert's school contains "automatic" prescriptions according to her students' performance profile. For instance, Jeremy, Margaret, and Megan mastered Topics 34 and 35, so their next assignment is to read pages 125 through 130 in their math text. Mike and Antonio, however, haven't mastered

FIGURE 4-2. NEW MATH PROGRAM

GROUP PROGRESS REPORT
WINSLOW SCHOOL
TEACHER: MRS. ALBERT
GROUP: MRS. ALBERT'S FIFTH GRADE
DATE: 11/18/83

NAME	TOPIC OBJECTIVES	34 1	2	35 1	2	3	36 1	2	37 1	2	38 1	2
Barrows, Jeremy		M	M	M	M	M	M	M	M	P	X	X
Duffy, Margaret		M	M	M	M	M	M	M	M	M	M	P
Hilton, Megan		M	M	M	M	M	P	P	P	X	X	X
Perez, Antonio		M	M	M	P	P	M	M	P	P	X	X
Yancy, Mike		M	M	M	M	P	P	X	X	X	X	X
NONMASTERY TOTALS		0	0	0	1	2	2	2	3	4	4	4

Topic 35, so they are assigned some practice problems in their supplementary workbook. Not all CMI systems are equipped to handle diagnosis and prescription in such a routine way. Instead, prescription is based on teacher interpretation of how students performed on prerequisite topics. In almost all cases, diagnosis is not diagnosis in the clinical sense. In other words, CMI systems don't yield diagnostic information that explains why students performed as their scores indicate. The information is simply a status report; it becomes your responsibility to assess the reasons for this performance and to determine appropriate instructional activities for the next assignment. As we become more experienced and sophisticated with CMI systems, perhaps we can build the "why" into the diagnostic component.

FIGURE 4-3. NEW MATH PROGRAM

INSTRUCTIONAL GROUPING REPORT
WINSLOW SCHOOL
TEACHER: MRS. ALBERT
INSTRUCTIONAL GROUPS FOR: TOPICS 35, 36
DATE: 11/18/83

TOPIC 35: ANGLES AND SYMMETRY

TOPIC 36: NUMBERS 0-999

NAME	TOPIC	35	36
Barrows, Jeremy		M	M
Duffy, Margaret		M	M
Hilton, Megan		M	P

Testing and Scoring Student Performance

An extremely time-consuming task for most teachers is the testing and grading of students' work. This is an area in which teachers especially appreciate the power of the computer. The CMI system Mrs. Albert uses can store many test items on a single topic, present on the computer screen an individualized test that has been randomly produced from the bank of test items, instantaneously score the test, and enter the score in the student's file. Other CMI systems don't have the testing feature so the teacher administers a test, then enters the data into the computer. Typical ways of getting this information into the computer are by keyboard entry and test scanner devices. Either way, the computer immediately updates the student's file to reflect these test results.

FIGURE 4-4. NEW MATH PROGRAM

DIAGNOSIS AND PRESCRIPTION REPORT
WINSLOW SCHOOL
TEACHER: MRS. ALBERT
GROUP: MRS. ALBERT'S FIFTH GRADE
DIAGNOSIS AND PRESCRIPTION FOR: TOPICS 34, 35
DATE: 11/18/83

NAME	TOPIC 34	35	PRESCRIPTION
Barrows, Jeremy	M	M	Read pp. 125-130 in math text
Duffy, Margaret	M	M	Read pp. 125-130 in math text
Hilton, Megan	M	M	Read pp. 125-130 in math text
Perez, Antonio	M	P	Do practice problems 1-10, p. 95 in *Math Wizards* book
Yancy, Mike	M	P	Do practice problems 1-10, p. 95 in *Math Wizards* book

---

Handling Instructional and Administrative Changes in the Program

Although some of the data in a CMI system are regarded as fixed, there are times when this information needs to be updated. Mrs. Albert received two new students during the last reporting period, and Mike Yancy moved to another district. The school's CMI system can make these changes simply by entering them into the computer via keyboard. Also, Mrs. Albert decided to add two objectives to Topic 36. An updated Group Progress Report, illustrated in Figure 4-5, shows the deletion of Mike Yancy, the performance of the class (including the two new students), and data regarding the additional objectives.

In the hypothetical scenario described above, Mrs. Albert quickly admits that the computer has not eliminated her management activities in the classroom. But her role as instructional manager has changed from collector, keeper, and reporter of information to manager of instructional decisions affecting both the immediate and long-range program goals of her students. Mrs. Albert spends more time thinking about instructional decisions and less time with the mechanics of management, something the computer handles with ease.

POINTS TO PONDER IN CONSIDERING A CMI SYSTEM

The image of the computer rescuing the embattled teacher from the mountain of paperwork is realistic ... to a point. The point is, computer managed instruction is not for everyone. To bill CMI as a panacea to your instructional management dilemma is to engage in outright deceit. Even though all of us want relief from tiresome management responsibilities, we must face the reality that effective computer managed instruction can only occur under certain conditions. This section highlights the considerations you should entertain as you contemplate developing or purchasing a CMI system.

Does Your Program Philosophy Match the Philosophy Underlying CMI?

As stated earlier in the chapter, CMI as a concept contains three underlying assumptions. The first assumption is that mastery learning is a desirable curriculum feature. Students pursue an instructional objective until they demonstrate mastery of it. Only then (within reason) can they move to the next objective in the unit. A second assumption is individualized instruction. In such a program, the curriculum is organized so that students move through the course at a pace dictated by individual abilities. Other factors affecting individualization include student interest, styles of learning and background experiences. The third assumption centers on the teacher as instruction manager. Instead of the teacher being consumed by endless clerical tasks, in CMI systems the teacher's role shifts to instructional decision-maker, with the computer taking up the slack in routine management functions.

If the foundation of your curriculum contains these elements, then CMI is worth considering. If the curriculum is based on large-group instruction, presented to all students at the same time, and if success in learning is relative to how other students perform on identical tasks, then you may be hard pressed to justify a move to computer managed instruction. This is particularly true if your instructional decisions aren't based on data that can be expressed in a quantifiable way.

Is Your Curriculum Structure Organized Sequentially?

Inherent in the assumptions of CMI is the stipulation that curriculum should be organized in a hierarchical way. That is, each unit of instruction serves as a stepping stone to higher levels of learning. Teachers have a clearly marked roadmap showing where students should go, based on where they've been. Ideally, in CMI systems, curriculum goals will differ, depending on individual differences. In practice, the goals are usually the same for all students, and they travel the same path to reach the goals, even though their individual paces will vary. If your curriculum can't be translated into clearly defined units of instruction, interconnected in some systematic way, it is unlikely a CMI system will prove useful. To be effective, the computer must have linear, step-by-step instructions to follow. Remove this sequential curriculum structure, and the teacher must rely strictly on personal judgment in managing classroom data.

Is Your Instructional Cycle Defined Sequentially?

Even though your curriculum may be structured in a linear fashion, the same question needs to be asked about your instructional cycle. By this term, we mean the process that students experience as they learn a segment of curriculum. As an example, a typical instructional cycle for teaching two-digit addition is to first assess how much the student knows, then prescribe appropriate instructional activities, and finally monitor his or her progress

FIGURE 4-5. NEW MATH PROGRAM

NAME	TOPIC OBJECTIVES	34 1	2	35 1	2	3	36 1	2	3	4
GROUP PROGRESS REPORT WINSLOW SCHOOL TEACHER: MRS. ALBERT GROUP: MRS. ALBERT'S FIFTH GRADE DATE: 11/25/83										
Barrows, Jeremy		M	M	M	M	M	M	M	M	P
Duffy, Margaret		M	M	M	M	M	M	M	P	P
Eckland, Cecille		M	M	M	M	P	P	X	X	X
Hilton, Megan		M	M	M	M	M	M	M	P	P
Perez, Antonio		M	M	M	P	P	X	P	X	
Sallstrom, Edgar		M	M	M	P	P	X	X	X	X
NONMASTERY TOTALS		0	0	0	1	3	3	3	5	6

toward the objective. CMI systems can be quite helpful in managing this kind of information. If, on the other hand, you don't have a predetermined pattern for your instructional process, it's impossible for the computer to guess what you want the students to do next.

Do Your Instructional Management Needs Require Computer Support?

Collecting, storing, analyzing, and reporting data in an individualized, mastery learning curriculum creates a management burden for the classroom teacher. If you are in this position, computer power can handle the manipulation of information while you handle instructional decision-making based on the computer-supplied information. If you rely almost exclusively on observation, personal judgment, and your mental notes on student performance as a basis for diagnosing, prescribing, and reporting, you may not have sufficient quantifiable information to justify a CMI system.

Can You Justify the Costs of a CMI System?

No precise formula exists for calculating the costs associated with a CMI system. In fact, the cost factor becomes more complicated when you consider costs associated with the amount of computer time available per student. General guidelines, however, can be applied to give you an idea of the expenses involved in implementing Computer Managed Instruction. Costs can be broken down into two categories, developmental and maintenance costs. If you choose to write your own CMI curriculum, you incur the personnel expense of curriculum development, as well as the expense of buying technical expertise to write the computer program supporting the curriculum. Estimates of this cost range from $50,000 to well over $100,000, depending on the scope of the project you undertake. An alternative to local curriculum development is to purchase your curriculum commercially. Because the commercial vendor can spread these development costs across many buyers, your outlay may be less than the cost of local development. But then you are faced with the prospect that the "canned" curriculum may not adequately meet your needs.

Once you've resolved the costs of development, you must deal with maintenance costs. These expenses can appear in various disguises. For example, maintenance of computer equipment might be performed by trained technicians employed by the school district. The expense, then, becomes time sacrificed in other areas to attend to the computer equipment. Another maintenance cost occurs when you decide to modify either the educational component or the computer component of the CMI system. If you choose to modify curriculum, you incur personnel costs in the form of curriculum development and computer program modification. If a decision is made to have more or different computerized reports, additional maintenance costs must be accounted for. As a final example, all of the information put into the computer must be entered by someone. Because this information constantly changes as students move through the curriculum, there is a constant demand for entering these data into computer memory. The costs associated with this task will vary, depending on how you allocate resources to perform this function—for example, teacher, aide, parent-volunteer.

The issue of costs to develop and maintain an effective CMI system should not be the overriding factor in considering Computer Managed Instruction. Realistically, though, a decision to implement a CMI system carries with it a price tag in addition to the costs incurred in the conventional curriculum.

CMI IN ACTION: TWO CASE STUDIES

It's one thing to talk theoretically about important ingredients in a successful CMI system. It's more instructive, however, to study actual examples of schools that have successfully overcome the obstacles and put CMI into practice. Two nationally acclaimed CMI projects are highlighted below.

Sherman School Project

One of the pioneers in Computer Managed Instruction in Sherman Elementary School in Madison, Wisconsin. The Sherman School Project grew out of a move in 1969 by the fourth- and fifth-grade teachers to individualize their mathematics program. Following is an account of the project as viewed by the team leader, Mrs. Berdella Grass:

> We began our project with 165 children in the fourth and fifth grade, six teachers, and an aide, housed in six traditional classrooms on a single corridor. During the scheduled time for math (45 minutes, five days per week), we kept the doors open and used the rooms as six separate stations: testing, prescription, seminar, quiz, game, and study rooms. Students moved freely among rooms according to the nature of their activities. Each teacher assumed a specific task for a week, then rotated

assignments. Even though we loved our new system, we needed help. Teachers were growing weary from the efforts needed to individualize the program. Students were growing impatient from having to wait in line at almost every station. The management component was growing burdensome from all the demands for recordkeeping. After contact with staff members at the University of Wisconsin, the Sherman School Project Team decided to computerize their mathematics program, beginning in the 1973-74 school year.

The transition did not come easy. With a lot of work to do, we eased into our project called MICA (Managed Instruction with Computer Assistance). Backed by a combination of Federal grants and school district funds totaling about $250,000, we computerized our individualized mathematics curriculum. Operationally, this meant that the curriculum was organized into 30 instructional units, with about 9 to 12 objectives in each unit. Our curriculum plan had a linear structure, with all students proceeding from study guide 1 to study guide 30. Within this plan, many of the math concepts and skills appeared at multiple points in the curriculum to consolidate skills, add sophistication to the concept, and provide review. The instructional model we used followed the sequence of pretest, diagnosis, prescription, instruction, and post test, with a heavy emphasis on diagnosis and prescription.

During the next two years, we streamlined our program, working out the "bugs" we encountered as we went along. By the third year of the Sherman School Project, we felt like we had achieved our goals. Teachers were free to do what they do best—teach. No more searching for prescriptions; no more writing student activities on 3x5 cards; no more long hours at home preparing assignments, correcting papers, and recording information. Both students and teachers were excited about this new venture.

Little did we know that the end of Federal funding would spell doom for the project. At the Board of Education Meeting on August 16, 1976, CMI in Madison came to a screeching halt on a 4-3 vote by the Board. They gave a variety of reasons, the chief one being "high" costs and a lack of evidence that the program produced better pupil performance when compared to other ways of individualizing instruction.

Even though the Sherman School Project no longer had computer support, the individualized mathematics program continued for some time. And all of the efforts by the Sherman staff were not totally lost. The McFarland (Wisconsin) Elementary School Project, described next, capitalized on the experiences gained through the Sherman School Project.

McFarland Project

Unlike the Sherman School vignette, the CMI project at McFarland is alive and well. Dr. Donald Barnes, principal at McFarland Elementary, describes the school's experience.

The elementary school in McFarland, Wisconsin started developing a computer-managed instructional system in 1973. The school had a commitment to team teaching, individualized instruction, and continuous progress since 1970 with the implementation of Individually Guided Education (IGE).

The first system started by the school took the form of manually recording skill mastery by means of a large chart. The process became so cumbersome to the teachers and aides that volunteers were sought to assist in recording. The staff soon found this to cause problems with the confidentiality of student records. Subsequently, contact was made with the University of Wisconsin Research and Development Center to begin a program of computer-managed instruction.

Our teachers were involved from the outset in the development of the CMI project. Each curriculum area we included had to be reviewed and sometimes rewritten. We took advantage of inservice days and extended employment during the summer to perform the necessary curriculum development. Originally, most of the funding for the McFarland Project came from federal grants. When these funds ended, the school district included our project within the school district budget. Costs to the district were the purchase of computer equipment, one-tenth of a teacher's salary to supervise the project, teacher-aide time, plus the usual costs associated with maintaining a CMI project.

Since 1973, the CMI system has developed into much more than planned initially. For example, the individualized student record can assist a staff member in a parent-teacher conference. Another benefit is the capability to cross-reference specific skills. For instance, if a graphing skill is mastered in mathematics, the record is updated in science and social studies where that skill appears. So we achieved the originally planned purpose of recordkeeping, grouping for teaching skills, and skill identification—and then some.

Our original computer system operated via a telephone hookup with a mainframe computer at the university. After five years, the school purchased a microcomputer for $15,000 to be housed in the school. The computer is used solely for computer managed instruction. This gives instruction a first priority. In fact, the school was cautioned about using the same computer for bookkeeping because the latter may take priority during pay periods.

Currently, the CMI curriculum consists of reading skills, mathematics, science, reference skills, the study skills section of social studies, and swimming. Each instructional unit is objective-based. We follow the instructional pattern of pretest, diagnosis, prescription, instruction, and post test. A record is kept of each student's progress. As he or she takes a test on a unit, the test information is recorded via scanner and immediately entered into the student's file.

The most outstanding benefit of our CMI curriculum is that it allows the teaching staff to be efficient in teaching. Skills being taught are identified, tested, and recorded. The system allows for individual instruction in terms of small to medium-sized groups.

The teaching staff at McFarland Elementary would find it difficult to return to the previous type of instruction—still, we have a lot to do. For example, we're interested in connecting Computer Assisted Instruction to our current management system. Also we would like to establish minimum standards for each grade level and enter them into the computer. In summary, even though we have come a long way with CMI, we feel we've just scratched the surface. We're definitely excited about the future.

The questions and case studies posed above do not purport to represent all issues you'll ever face in considering a CMI system. They do represent, however, important questions that deserve attention before you proceed further in contemplating a CMI system. In fact, computer managed instruction is not the only management application available to schools. Chapter 5 shows how computer power can be put to work in managing administrative functions.

CHAPTER 4 REFERENCES

Allen, M., "Computer Managed Instruction," *Journal of Research and Development in Education*, Fall 1980.

Baker, F., *Computer Managed Instruction: Theory and Practice*, Englewood Cliffs, NJ: Educational Technology Publications, Inc., 1978.

Chapin, J., *An Administrative Summary of the Madison Metropolitan School District's E.S.E.A. Title III Computer Managed Instruction Program: MICA*, Madison, WI, unpublished manuscript, 1977.

Crouse, D. B., "The Computerized Gradebook as a Component of a Computer Managed Curriculum," *Educational Technology*, May 1981.

Gundlach, A., "Managing Instruction with a Micro," *Educational Computer*, May/June 1981.

Leiblum, M., "Computer Managed Instruction: An Explanation and Overview," *AEDS Journal*, Spring 1982.

McIsaac, D., and F. Baker, "Computer Managed Instruction System Implementation on a Microcomputer," *Educational Technology*, Oct. 1981.

Spuck, D., et al., *Evaluation of the Wisconsin System for Instructional Management (WIS-SIM Pilot Test)*, Madison, WI: Wisconsin Research and Development Center, Technical Report No. 438, 1977.

TAPPING THE POWER OF THE COMPUTER AS ADMINISTRATIVE ASSISTANT

The sleek, stylish image of an "office of tomorrow" graces the front cover of many contemporary business magazines. Inside, articles foretell the time when executive work stations will have everything needed to hold long-distance meetings, transmit reports to another state instantaneously, request up-to-the-minute sales performance of personnel, and dictate letters that are instantly printed and ready for mailing. Even today, a typical business office houses the necessary technology to computerize a wide variety of administrative functions, including payroll, budget, sales forecasts, personnel files, and word processing. In education, we have similar applications of computer technology ready and waiting for our use. Chapter 5 introduces you to the wealth of administrative applications via computer technology. You also will be provided with guidelines to help you decide which of these uses are most appropriate for your situation.

PUTTING A MANAGEMENT INFORMATION SYSTEM
TO WORK IN SCHOOLS

Just as in education, the business world has its own set of jargon, shorthand expressions for more complex ideas. For instance, the concept of using a computer to collect, store, and retrieve information is commonly referred to as a data base management system (DBMS) or a management information system (MIS). Essentially, such a system consists of important, frequently used information, and a computer program to transform the various pieces of information into meaningful records. From computerized school district bus routes that optimize costs, total distance traveled, number of routes formed, and energy consumed, to a report listing parents' hobbies for an elementary school, an MIS serves as an invaluable administrative assistant. The key is first to understand how an MIS can be applied, then decide priority areas for its use.

COMPUTERIZING STUDENT FILES

You won't spend very much time in a school office today before discovering the pile of reports to be done. It seems that various agencies need similar (not the **same**) information on students. One way of streamlining report production is to implement an MIS. In doing this, you create an electronic filing cabinet that can be opened at your request. Imagine the equivalent of three file drawers of student information stored on a couple of computer disks. Imagine, also, the ability to find pertinent files in a matter of seconds. A computerized MIS lets you find and manipulate student information to yield the type of report being requested at the moment. To illustrate what an MIS can do, let's create a file for a student we'll call Dixie Lee Morris. Dixie Lee's father completed the school's annual questionnaire shown in Figure 5-1. This information was entered into the MIS by computer keyboard. For Dixie Lee's file, the secretary simply needed to update the information on file from last year. Assuming adequate computer capabilities and an appropriately designed computer program, you can compile a wide variety of reports just from the information on the annual questionnaire. Representative reports from this hypothetical MIS include:

- alphabetical listing of all seniors
- families grouped by census tract
- seniors rank-ordered by age
- mailing labels to the parents of all seniors
- students with allergies
- listing of unimmunized students
- students who ride the bus to school
- all girls currently playing soccer on the school's team

Drawing from the annual questionnaire alone, many more reports could be generated. To get these reports, you simply tell the computer program which categories you need from the student file, and give instructions about how this information should be formatted.

Combining the student file with other information in the electronic filing cabinet, you can produce an even wider range of reports. Suppose, for instance, you have separate files on attendance, standardized test scores, and quarterly grade reports. Conceivably you could request the MIS to generate the following reports:

- all students absent more than 15 days this quarter
- students scoring above the 90th percentile on the recent standardized test but whose grades were below a "C" average
- a count of absences for students riding the school bus

By merging the information contained in the separate files, a computerized MIS gives you the power to take bits of information from various files and produce required student reports faster than you can roll your chair to the metal filing cabinet.

USING AN MIS TO MANAGE BUSINESS OPERATIONS

The same principles used for producing student reports can be applied in other administrative areas. For most of us, little

FIGURE 5-1. STUDENT QUESTIONNAIRE, HAWTHORNE HIGH SCHOOL

Student Name: Morris, Dixie Lee

Date of Birth: 9/1/65

Sex: Female

Current Grade: 12

Address: 2009 Broadway Court 03771

Phone: 555-1171 (home)   555-1486 (office—father)

Census Tract: 012

Father's Name: Morris, Christopher J.

Father's Address: Same

Mother's Name: Morris, Cheryl A.

Mother's Address: Same

Siblings: (name, age, and grade) Mark—11, 7th grade

Emergency Contact: George or Susan Anthony
                   1908 Broadway Court
                   555-2100

Medical Record: Allergies—cats, dust
                Immunization—compliance

School Transportation: Metro Bus

School Sports Program: _____ baseball   ___x___ soccer

                       _____ basketball   _____ football

thought goes into the process for generating paychecks and payroll reports. Consider, though, how an MIS can perform a valuable service in calculating and producing paychecks. Suppose, at your school, every staff member has a file (similar to a student file) containing information like salary schedule, days worked, payroll deductions, and exemptions. Each payroll period, the computer automatically figures your salary based on the data in your file and prints your checks accordingly. Information from these files can also be used to prepare the payroll reports. Other sample personnel functions performed by an MIS include:

- an individual's employment history in the school district
- seniority list for all teachers
- staff directories
- a list of all teachers in a specified salary range
- salary schedule simulation during contract negotiations

Another area becoming incorporated into contemporary MIS systems is the domain of facilities and equipment. Obvious examples of these reports are computerized equipment inventories and energy consumption tables. A less obvious but equally important use is in projecting future space needs. It's possible, for example, to store school information in such categories as enrollment patterns, student capacity, number of students within walking distance, and operational costs per square foot. The computer can use these variables to give you projected enrollment by grade level, efficiency quotients regarding use of space, and the projected need for busing service. This application of a Management Information System does two things: it accomplishes in seconds what would take weeks to calculate manually, and it gives you the most reliable estimate possible for planning future facility requirements.

One of the earliest forms of an MIS in school districts was in financial applications. Because of the need for speed, accuracy, and reliability in its accounting procedures, schools have the opportunity to automate functions like:

- general accounting
- expenditure and revenue forecasting
- accounts receivable and payable
- purchase orders

Other, specialized uses of financial information can be built into an MIS according to local needs. Without attempting to provide a complete list of all administrative applications, this section has highlighted some ways a school can employ an MIS to more efficiently manage many of its administrative functions.

MANAGING THE EDUCATIONAL PROGRAM
WITH THE HELP OF COMPUTERS

Not too long ago, all administrative tasks associated with managing the school had to be done manually. Now things have changed. The school administrator can enlist the help of computers in managing a wide range of educational functions. Because of the steady influx of new applications, any attempt to provide a definitive list entails the risk of producing an obsolete list before it appears in print. Instead, this section samples the smorgasbord of educational applications by highlighting three areas in which computers demonstrate their strength in managing the educational program.

A time-consuming task for teachers is the periodic labor of completing student report cards. Computer programs can come to the rescue by automating certain steps in the process. To illustrate, unhappy with existing procedures, the staff members of one middle school decided they wanted a report card system (Patterson et al., 1976) that:

- allows each teacher to establish a pool of comments for each course
- provides annual progress information for each student on a single document
- reduces the tedious task of writing comments
- helps assure a fair evaluation of all students

In response to this request, central office technicians designed a computerized report card system (see Figure 5-2) with the following characteristics.

Comments. Each course has a pool of 24 comments written by the teacher, who selects up to four comments for every student in the course. The teacher has the flexibility to change, add, or delete specific comments as needed. In other words, the content of each comment is the individual teacher's prerogative.

Achievement Grade Levels. A maximum of seven achievement grade levels can be selected. In the case of the middle school just mentioned, teachers chose these designations: excellent, above

FIGURE 5-2. COMPUTERIZED PUPIL PROGRESS REPORT

	HALF DAYS ABSENT		TIMES TARDY	
	QUARTER	YEAR	QUARTER	YEAR
	1	83/84	2	83/84

STUDENT NAME	NUMBER
PENNINGTON, REHNA	694103

QUARTER	SCHOOL YEAR
2	83/84

GRADE 06   HOMEROOM

COURSE/INSTRUCTOR	PROGRESS LEVEL	COMMENTS
1006-01 LANG ARTS 6 O'Rourke	Excellent	Spelling Tests—Excellent Written Expression—Very Good Effort—Very Good Fine contributions to class discussions
1036-01 READING 6 O'Rourke	Above Average	Good Effort Comprehension Progress—Good Vocabulary Development—Good Good Book Reviews/Reports
2006-01 SPECIAL STUDIES 6 O'Rourke	Above Average	Good class discussion Good work on projects Daily work—Good Effort—Good

MATH 6 Harper	3006-01	Excellent	**Good Test Results** Shows willingness to check and correct work Successfully attempted enrichment work
SCIENCE 6 Harper	4006-01	Excellent	**Good Test Results** Needs to improve research skills Interprets science materials effectively
PHY ED 6 Zahn	5016-03	Average	Average Skill Level—in Soccer Average Skill Level—in Touch Football
BAND 6 Kaiser	7106-01	Excellent	A pleasure to have in class
IND ED 6 Connors	9006-04	Excellent	Does quality work Follows directions well Is reliable and responsible

ACHIEVEMENT GRADE LEVELS

1-Excellent	2-Above Average	3-Average
4-Below Average	5-Failing	6-Medical Excuse 7-Incomplete

average, average, below average, medical excuse, failing, and incomplete.

Course Master. Each year, a master file is established of all courses to be graded. This file includes the course number, section number, instructor, and quarter to be graded. A maintenance procedure allows the teacher or administrator to add courses, change any information about a course, and delete courses.

Pupil Progress Report. At the end of each quarter, the computer prints a scan sheet for each class, and the teacher marks the sheets with an achievement grade level and up to four comments for each student. Next, the computer consolidates all scan sheets from teachers and prints one progress report for each student. The report can be printed in a variety of sequences, such as student number and homeroom, to facilitate distribution.

Class Report. Each teacher receives a class list containing the grades and comments for each student in the class. This report presents, in concise form, a record of all students for the quarter.

In a survey regarding the acceptance of this computerized grade reporting system, parents, students, and teachers overwhelmingly endorsed the plan. Parents felt the report was easy to understand and that the comments section was sufficiently definitive. Teachers said the computerized system was a fast, efficient method of communicating student progress without depersonalizing the teacher-student-parent relationship.

Scheduling is another area in which computers help manage the educational program. Administrators who manually schedule each student's classes find it virtually impossible to keep in mind variables like parent requests, teacher notes to separate certain students, lunch periods, and class balance according to sex, ability, level, and cultural and ethnic diversity. Complicating this juggling act is the inevitable entry and withdrawal of students as schedules are being built. The computer can store the variables you need to consider, and can automatically update class schedules as students come and go. In scheduling classes at the secondary level, the computer can take the rank order preferences of students and build a schedule optimizing the choices for the student population.

FIGURE 5-3. 33 WAYS TO USE COMPUTERS IN THE LIBRARY*

1. *Word Processing.* Commercially available word processing programs provide the ability rapidly to produce error-free letters, reports, and other documents. Documents needing periodic revision need not be completely retyped. Words, lines, or paragraphs may be changed, deleted, or replaced with minimum effort. Abbreviations for common words or phrases used in keyboarding may be easily expanded. Word processor programs can be used as input data collectors for other library programs, and for editing the output of other programs. A microcomputer with a good word processor not only may cost less than dedicated word processing equipment, but provides a flexible machine which can be used for many other purposes as well. We strongly recommend that the first step a library should take on the acquisition of a microcomputer is the purchase of a good word processing program. In fact, many of the applications listed below can be carried out using a word processor alone—perhaps not as efficiently as with special-purpose programs, but much more efficiently than by manual methods.

2. *Catalog Card Typing.* The computer prompts for the basic parts of a catalog card, then types a card set onto the proper card stock in fanfold form. Our programs permit saving the cataloging data for later use for acquisitions lists, subject bibliographies, selective dissemination, and other purposes. Program prompts make sure that data elements that should be included are included. AACR2 punctuation, expansion of abbreviations, and some data elements ("cm." for size and "LC" preceding Library of Congress card numbers, for example) are automatically supplied by the program set.

3. *Union Lists.* The computer provides a means for easy data collection, printout, and updating of union lists of periodicals for local areas, school and public libraries in a city or town, for example. Provision for recording new holdings and locations, for printout by location, and for computer search of files may easily be incorporated.

4. *Union Catalogs.* A union catalog among various agencies can be implemented. If disk space or keyboarding costs prevent full

entries, then Library of Congress card numbers with locations can still provide an extremely useful resource. Such a catalog need not cover retrospective materials, but can be quite useful if started and maintained on a day-forward basis for new titles and currently requested materials.

5. *Bibliographic Listings.* Programs can provide for a broad variety of types of bibliographies, producing a main listing with space for annotations, etc., and offer the possibility of a variety of indexes or index entry types: author, title, subject, and classes.

6. *Newspaper Indexing.* Programs can provide for index production, cumulations, editing, and computer search of material not yet printed out. We have just completed such a program set for the North Carolina State Library and will make it available for wider distribution.

7. *General Indexing.* Microcomputers can be useful for the rapid production and revision of indexes to books, documents, reports, manuals, and handbooks. Our program set for this purpose has seen very heavy use in producing indexes for books published by, for instance, Holt, Rinehart and the American Library Association. Most recently, it is in use by the British Library to index staff manuals, and by the North Carolina State Library to index state documents. A paper describing our general indexing program set has been published in the *Indexer*, the journal of the British and American Societies of Indexers.

8. *Rapid Reference File.* A novel concept that is very interesting to us is that of maintaining a computer-searchable file of past reference questions and sources for answers and—where the answers are brief—of the answers themselves. Records of the cumulative frequency and last date of each request may be used to keep the file up to date and to keep its size reasonable. Our preliminary research indicates that reference questions tend to be highly repetitive within libraries and probably across various libraries of the same type. Such files, therefore, may not only be useful in themselves, but could lead to the development of new reference tools, either in book or machine-readable form. There are a number of commercially available data base programs that would seem suitable for this purpose.

9. *Subject and Name Authority Files and Thesauri.* Subject and name authority files and thesauri may be easily compiled and maintained by microcomputer. Data for input can be derived from microcomputer based catalogs and indexes without the need for rekeyboarding, and may be edited using a word processing program. An extensive (20-page) paper describing our novel combination of features from both thesauri and subject heading lists, plus new concepts as applied to headings for children's materials, is available from us for the cost of photocopying. Computer based lists of this kind can provide new means of access to collections.

10. *Internal Report Literature Control, Abstracting Services.* Many special libraries, including those with access to large computer systems, have difficulty in getting adequate control of their internal report literature, given the difficulties of explaining needs to systems people and of being sure of having consistent access to the big computers. Microcomputers can provide control of internal report literature in special libraries. We have developed a system that permits production of an abstracting service for these (or other) materials, which provides for cumulative indexes, and for computer search for information not yet printed out.

11. *Vertical File Heading Lists.* The computer provides an easy way of maintaining vertical file heading lists and producing up-to-date copies for patrons and staff. Cross-reference cards for the catalog for vertical file subjects can be produced, as can such headings for a COM catalog.

12. *Information and Referral Services.* The computer can be used for directory compilation, easy updating, and computer search of information on local, state, regional, and national agencies and services.

13. *Film Bookings, Room Scheduling, and Other Similar Activities.* Again, the computer can maintain, update, and search schedules of this nature. Statistics on room or media use can be generated from the schedule data. Here, it may well be possible to use one of the commercially available data base programs for this purpose.

14. *Local Events Calendars.* Suitable programs can collect data for a local events calendar, providing for printout in a form

suitable for duplication and for computer search. Again, a commercially available data base program could be adapted to this use.

15. *Community Resource Directory.* Computer programs can be used for directory compilation, updating, and computer search for information and resource persons and agencies in the community.

16. *Telephone and Address Directories.* In addition to production of the lists in a form suitable for reproduction, appropriate programs can print address labels and permit computer search of the files. The data can be used with some word processing program sets to generate form letters, overdues, etc.

17. *Library Statistics.* Statistics of circulation, reference questions, interlibrary loan and similar activities can be generated and kept using the computer. If data are entered on a weekly or monthly basis, statistics can easily be generated for that time frame, as well as for year-to-date and other cumulations.

18. *Inventories.* General data base programs can be easily used to maintain inventory-type lists. An equipment inventory data base could include information such as serial number, warranty date, replacement lamps, service sources, and date of last servicing.

19. *Special Collections.* Creating a data base for special collections, such as a local history collection, can serve many purposes. Information can be entered so that catalog cards, a book catalog (which could be published), and selected annotated bibliographies can all be generated from one keyboarding. We have developed programs for calendaring archives, which provide semi-automatic indexing for the calendar—admittedly a very specialized application, but one we think is important.

20. *Overdues and Patron Lists.* For libraries using Gaylord (or similar) charging systems, the borrower record file by borrower number can be maintained as a computer-searchable file, and this file used in the production of overdue notices. If the computer is simply used to enter new borrower information and to do overdues on a day-forward basis, most borrowers who will turn up in overdues will soon be on record without excessive keyboarding costs.

21. *Ordering.* While we have said that we were excluding strictly business applications from this list, ordering is included

because cataloging data are available for so many titles at the time of ordering, and may be captured as part of the ordering process. An ordering program can maintain budget statistics, produce order sheets or slips, and pass cataloging information to other programs.

22. *Reserves*. Computer programs may be used both to expedite reserves on individual books to patrons, and to maintain reserve lists for class assignments. In the latter case, not only can lists by class be supplied, but the computer can provide lists in shelf-list order for getting materials from the shelves or for easy identification of materials.

23. *Selective Dissemination of Information*. Computer programs can maintain a profile of borrower interests, match them against newly acquired titles, and notify borrowers of new material likely to be of particular interest. The same profiles can be most useful in forming acquisitions policies. [cite Peter Hiatt]

24. *Title Derivative (Permuted Title, KWOC, KWIC) Indexes*. Indexes of this kind can be most useful for materials that have not been fully cataloged—filmstrips and 16mm files in schools are a good example, particularly since their titles tend to be quite descriptive. Such indexes enter each item under each significant word in the title.

25. *Community Bulletin Boards*. Many microcomputer user groups maintain interactive bulletin board facilities for want ads, electronic mail, and other purposes. Library sponsorship and maintainance of such a utility could be quite valuable—to serve the growing public who have computers of their own, as well as a good way to get involved with user groups, which can be quite helpful with computing problems.

26. *Interlibrary Loan*. A microcomputer with modem (telephone) linkage to other libraries can expedite interlibrary loan.

27. *Commercial Information Facilities*. While some libraries might consider such services as those provided by Orbit, Dialog, or BRS as being too expensive—at least for the moment—there are other information utilities such as the Source or CompuServe that are quite inexpensive during off-prime time, which can provide valuable user services. Microcomputers with modems can serve as intelligent terminals for such facilities.

28. *Periodicals and Annuals.* Microcomputers can be used to generate orders for such materials, for checking in periodicals, and for generating claims for missing issues.

29. *Car Pools.* A number of libraries handle the arrangement of car pools as a public service. Microcomputer programs can aid in such an activity.

30. *Readability Measurement.* Microcomputer programs may be used to apply a variety of readability formulae, or for the production of Cloze text. We have written a number of such programs.

31. *Table of Contents Services.* Locally produced table of contents services can be useful for informing staff or teachers about new articles of interest to them in the professional literature. The data collected can be accumulated for later search and for producing bibliographies.

32. *Indexing Groups of Periodicals or the Literature of a Subject.* We have written programs that produce indexes in a format similar to that used by the Wilson Company for, say, *Library Literature* or the *Reader's Guide.* These programs are highly economic and, if library-style subject headings were used, would permit periodical index articles to be merged with other library bibliographic lists.

33. *Data Collection for Other Computers.* Microcomputers can be used to collect data for larger systems or for other microcomputers. Data may be exchanged directly, by telephone, or by magnetic media such as disks.

---

*Source: Hines, T C., L. Winkel, R. Collins, and F. Harvey, "Library Applications of Microcomputers," Greensboro, NC: University of North Carolina at Greensboro, School of Education Report, 1982, pp. 2-5.

The school office is not the only place for harnessing computer power to help manage the school's educational program. Recently, a lot of attention has been devoted to computer applications in the school library. As funds become more scarce, library personnel continue looking for ways to maintain services. One option is to assign a lot of the clerical tasks to the computer, allowing the professional staff to attend to more important functions. A recent article (Hines et al., 1982) listed 33 ways to use computers in the library (see Figure 5-3). In the guidance office, the computer helps students in their choices regarding career or college. For instance, a student could specify an interest in a liberal arts college, located in the Midwest, with a student enrollment under 3,000. Additionally, the student could enter family income data. The computer prints out all colleges meeting these conditions, as well as available financial aid, based on the information the student supplies about his or her family.

As mentioned earlier, new ways will continue to appear for using computer power as an assistant to the administrator. Make sure you have explored the latest options before making your final decisions.

USING WORD PROCESSING TO
IMPROVE CLERICAL EFFICIENCY

A powerful application of the computer as administrative assistant can be found in the secretary's office. Computer programs now exist that can turn the computer into a word processing machine. Basically, word processors take the features of a typewriter, with added features that permit you to create, erase, modify, and change information on a TV-type screen, without printing anything until you are satisfied that the document is exactly as you want it to appear as a finished product. Some selling points for using the word processing capabilities of computers are that they:

- increase productivity in the office
- improve the quality of final documents
- reduce office costs
- free secretarial and executive time for more profitable activities

Although these claims aren't backed by years of extensive research, they are supported by anecdotal accounts pointing to improved effectiveness and efficiency. For example, a quick survey of business journals uncovers these testimonials that word processing:

- saves two minutes per page on original documents and eight minutes on revisions

- reduces preparation of lengthy, complicated legal documents from six hours to one hour
- allows the secretary to handle the work of five physicians instead of two
- cuts time typing reports by 50 percent

Even without research to substantiate the various praises offered in behalf of word processing, actual experience using word processing technology is in itself a convincing argument.

FIGURE 5-4. DRAFT OF LETTER

October 30, 1983

Mr. Vernon Anderson, Principal
Oaklawn High School
Owensboro, West Virginia

Dear Mr. Anderson:

This letter is in response to your request for a copy of our new student report card. Regretfully, we have to wait for final school board approval before we can distribute the form. As soon as this happens, I will send you a copy.

Thanks for your interest.

Sincerely,

Susan Stein, Principal
Bellevue High School

To illustrate some of the characteristics of word processing, let's examine a first draft of the letter shown in Figure 5-4. Keeping in mind that it's impossible to capture the dynamics of interactive typing between secretary and computer, imagine the following scenario: Dr. Stein, principal of Bellevue High School, reviews the first draft displayed on the screen and decides that the first sentence is too long and awkward, that the letter should be saved until the school board meets in two days, and that a sentence should be added at the end. Therefore, Dr. Stein asks the secretary to save the first draft on a computer disk. Three days later, after the school board meeting, the revised letter depicted in Figure 5-5 is printed and mailed. In making the revisions, the secretary transferred the draft from the disk to the computer screen, deleted the first part of the first sentence, changed the part about the school board, and added a sentence at the end of the letter. All of these changes took less than two minutes; the computer program adjusted all of the spacing and paragraphing due to changes; and the secretary printed a final copy from computer to printer, without having to retype the letter. In addition, the computer printed a mailing label using information from the inside address, so the secretary didn't even have to address the envelope.

FIGURE 5-5. FINAL COPY OF LETTER

November 15, 1983

Mr. Vernon Anderson, Principal
Oaklawn High School
Owensboro, West Virginia

Dear Mr. Anderson:

I am writing in response to your request for a copy of our new student report card. The school board just approved distribution of the form. Therefore, I'm enclosing a copy.

Thanks for your request. I will keep you posted on parent reactions to the new card.

Sincerely,

Susan Stein, Principal
Bellevue High School

The above example is just one of the many features of word processing. Other applications include compiling mailing lists, indexing, combining letters, preparing charts and other graphics on the screen, as well as producing personalized letters from a standard form stored on a disk in the office.

To fully appreciate what word processing can offer as an administrative assistant, you should arrange for a demonstration by someone already using this technology in a school setting. If this option isn't available, contact a local vendor for a show-and-tell session. In any case, serious consideration should be given to computerizing the typing functions in the office.

THINGS TO THINK ABOUT BEFORE DECIDING ON ADMINISTRATIVE APPLICATIONS

As appealing as the computer may seem for a variety of administrative uses, in the face of scarce resources, you may be forced to limit your choices to only the most critical needs. The following questions focus on several key questions you need to ask before deciding how the computer can best be used administratively.

Can the Tasks Be Better Handled Manually?

Not all administrative functions need to be computerized. Depending on the scope of the task, it may take less time to locate the information manually than it does to select the correct disk, load it into the computer, perform the necessary operations on the information, and print it in acceptable form. As an illustration, suppose you need to find out how many students are in each homeroom at your high school. A simple list of homeroom teachers on your bulletin board, showing the number of students written in the margin, makes an excellent log. As a student withdraws, you can update the log with the stroke of a pencil. If you maintained a computerized list, you would have to load the disk into the computer, make the change, and put away the disk. These procedures would need to be carried out each time a student entered or withdrew from school. As another example, imagine that you are required to maintain a daily count of how many students use the school lunch program. If a person in the lunchroom accounts for all students on line each day, you can manually transfer that information to your report more easily than you could take the same information, type it into the computer, and then print it out. So, before you become lured into automating everything, check to see if computerizing the administrative application does the following:

- saves time
- saves money
- yields more accurate data
- yields more detailed data
- assists in decision-making
- frees human energy for more productive activities

Is the Service Already Available Centrally?

A major problem with streamlining administrative functions through computer technology is the ensuing duplication of effort. Conceivably, each school could develop or purchase a computer program that produced payroll records. Perhaps, though, central office personnel already have the information stored on the district computer and can produce the necessary payroll records. All that may be required is coordinating your needs with their information base. As another illustration, suppose you want a listing of your staff by seniority. Rather than wasting energy trying to develop a program to accomplish this task, it may be easier to see if the personnel department keeps this information on file and can supply you with a printout for your school. Finally, before computerizing your standardized test scores, check to see if the district or the test publisher can produce the needed information for you. In particular, larger school districts central offices with their own computer have the capability to accommodate many administrative functions needed by the individual schools.

Will the Computer Improve Efficiency Without Expanding Activity?

This question may not be answered fully without some use of the computer on a pilot basis. In the business sector, administrators found many examples of technology increasing office activity at the expense of efficiency. The introduction of the high-speed copier is a glaring example. Office workers found their time wasted by copying volumes of printed matter that previously was not considered worth duplicating. A similar condition was created with the advent of word processors. Reports became more numerous, largely because of the ease in creating them via computers. In education, we should take heed. Before moving to the computerization of office procedures, we need to prove that it's necessary, without merely generating unneeded reports.

Which Administrative Applications Receive the Highest Priority?

Most likely you are going to see several competing administrative uses for the limited resources available. In such a case, you will be forced to rule out some desirable options. The librarian can build a strong case for using computers in managing the library; the secretary can demonstrate that using the word processing features of the computer will be cost effective; personnel and finance decisions can be made easier with the assistance of computer-generated reports. The issue, then, becomes deciding which applications you can support. The answer hinges on your ability to examine closely each application, according to criteria designed for your specific requirements.

Can You Justify Computer Technology in the Office When It Could Be Used in the Classroom?

The decision to put a computer in the office usually means also deciding not to spend money putting computers in the classroom. If the ultimate goal in using computers is improved learning, it may be difficult to justify an administrative application that doesn't directly accomplish this goal. On political grounds alone, you may be asked why you favor the computer's office functions over having the children use the equipment.

There is, however, another side to the story. Most schools don't earmark their entire budget for instructional purposes. Lunchroom supervision, office supplies, and teacher lounge furniture are just some of the items demanding a portion of the school budget. And these expenses don't ordinarily come under fire for draining the instructional budget. Besides, improved efficiency in the administrative arena frees the principal and secretary to spend more time on instructional matters. At any rate, this question should not be treated lightly as you consider using computers for management functions.

Answers to these and other questions you pose will help direct your decisions about which administrative applications can best benefit from computer technology. Once you reach a decision on administrative uses, you must then weigh these applications against other applications described earlier. Chapter 6 will guide you through the critical steps toward selecting the optimal distribution of computer technology in schools.

CHAPTER 5 REFERENCES

Akers, R., "Database Scorecard," *Microcomputing*, April, 1982.

Hansen, T., D. Klassen, and J. Lindsay, "Impact of Computer-Based Information Systems Upon School and School District Administration," *AEDS Journal*, Fall 1978.

Moursund, D., *School Administrator's Introduction to Instructional Use of Computers*, LaGrande, OR: International Council for Computers in Education, 1980.

Patterson, J., et al., "Computerized Report Cards," *Educational Technology*, Aug. 1976.

6

SELECTING
COMPUTER APPLICATIONS
YOU NEED THE MOST

Pretend, for a moment, that computers have become an educational priority nationwide and you have the luxury of ample resources to implement any computer application you consider cost effective. How will you decide to spend these resources? Or, following the more likely scenario of insufficient funds for all cost effective computer applications, how will you choose among those uses holding the highest priority? Whether you are flush with funds or pinching pennies, Chapter 6 guides you, step by step, through this decision-making process. You will have the opportunity to apply the criteria outlined below to each computer application as you decide which uses will receive the most attention.

CRITERIA FOR EVALUATING COMPUTER APPLICATIONS

In deciding which uses of computer technology are in the best interest of your school in general and of the kids in particular, it's helpful to apply common criteria to each computer application. By asking the same core questions each time, you will form a bank of objective data to use in comparing the various applications you are considering. From that point, other forces take over. Realistically, you will decide on computer use depending on a combination of objective information, subjective judgment, and the various political, economic, and social forces operating at the moment. Hopefully, your responses to the following criteria will weigh heavily in your decision.

What Is the Rationale for Using This Application?

In education, we aren't inclined to make decisions based on extensive field testing or pilot studies. Instead, we rely partially on researchers' information and largely on our own experience. In the real world of schools, we skip over comprehensive needs assessments that were designed to pinpoint our needs and to tell us how they can be met. Instead, we usually make program decisions based on a rationale that is grounded in research, theory, and practice. Proceeding on the assumption of what's best for kids, we ask questions about purpose and how the proposed innovation is better than what we currently have or do.

In considering the various computer applications, you can proceed similarly. Carefully review the previous material, the points outlined in this chapter, and other sources on the topic, making note of each application's strengths and shortcomings. This process should produce enough information for the data bank mentioned earlier. Drawing from this bank, you will have a grounded rationale for every computer application you wish to investigate further.

Where Can This Application Be Used Most Effectively?

Chances are great that you face the unpopular prospect of having to select some requests over others when it comes to putting computers in schools. One criterion for decision-making will probably be effectiveness, or more precisely, relative effectiveness. With each computer application, the number of potential users will outstrip the number of machines available. In deciding where the limited number of computers can be used most effectively, you may want to consider factors such as the research regarding effectiveness, the areas in which computers can be better instructors or managers, and the subject or grade levels having enthusiastic, trained teachers. Undoubtedly, you'll add your own factors. When you've answered this effectiveness question, you should have a better idea of where the computers will go in your educational program.

What Are the Costs Associated with This Application?

Whether we like it or not, the issue of costs plays an important role in deciding how to allocate resources. In estimating a budget for computer technology, the issue gets complicated by the assortment of hidden costs tacked on to up-front expenses. Clearly, hardware (equipment) expenses are main cost considerations. Equally significant but less prominent are software (computer program), maintenance, staff development, and repair costs. In trying to arrive at some "ball park" figure for an investment in computer technology, we need to make some gross assumptions. Realizing that these assumptions are subject to error and modification, according to your own local circumstances, the final numbers, as well as the process of arriving at them, will provide a basis for comparison across applications.

For instructional applications, CAL and computer literacy assume that the necessary computer equipment will cost $1,000 per package (even though your actual costs could be considerably lower—depending on the capabilities and quality of the equipment you choose). This package includes the computer, monitor, and accessories like the cassette recorder. Assume also that the lifespan of the equipment is three years. This doesn't mean the machines totally depreciate to salvage value over three years. It just means that you may use today's technology for about three years before replacing it with more advanced computers. Over this three-year span, assume that all other costs will equal the total hardware cost. In other words, for purposes of this discussion, calculate the three-year cost for software, maintenance, repair, and staff development at $1,000 for each computer. In summary, the three-year budget projection for each computer used for CAL and Computer Literacy should be $2,000 ($1,000 for equipment and $1,000 for all other costs).

Now that these ground rules have been laid for costs per unit, you need some method for determining total costs for each instructional application. The formula outlined in Figure 6-1 serves this purpose. Each variable in the formula is explained below.

FIGURE 6-1. FORMULA FOR CALCULATING COMPUTER TIME AVAILABLE PER STUDENT

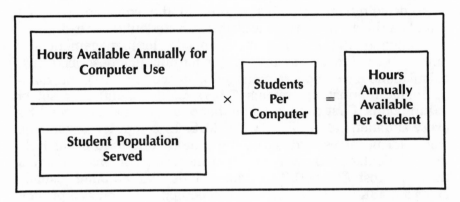

Number of Hours Available Annually for Computer Use. This figure is computed by multiplying the hours per school day, times the number of days per school year, times the percentage of time the computer will be used. Suppose your school day is six hours long and that you are in school 180 days a year. This translates into 1080 hours of instruction during the school year. Obviously, the computer won't be whirring and purring every hour of the year. School programs, class parties, lunch periods, field trips, and other activities take a bite out of the 1080 hours potentially available. Therefore, you need to estimate the percentage of time the computer will be turned on, and multiply this figure by 1080 hours to arrive at a realistic number of hours available annually for computer use.

Student Population Served. This figure can be the entire student enrollment at your school, the number of students in a particular subject, or how many students attend a special program, such as learning disabled students.

Students per Computer. Use an average figure for this calculation. That is, on the average, how many students at a time will use the computer for instructional purposes? In some classes, this figure may be steady at two students per computer. In other cases, from one to five students may get to use the computer together, depending on the application.

Hours Annually Available for Each Student. This figure represents the total hours for the year that each student gets to work on the computer. Again, this reflects an average. Some students may get considerably more time and some much less. After deciding on the other figures in the equation, you can calculate the average hours available per student, per year.

Since the number of computers needed for management isn't directly related to the variables in the formula just described, cost calculations for computer managed instruction (CMI) and management information systems (MIS) require a different set of assumptions. First of all, assume that one computer is needed for every situation calling for CMI or MIS. In computer jargon, the computer becomes a "dedicated" machine—one used exclusively for a particular purpose. For each of these applications, assume a hardware cost of $3,000. This price includes the computer (usually at least a 48K machine), plus related equipment such as a printer, two disk drives, and a monitor. The related costs, particularly software, vary considerably depending on each application. Therefore, elaboration on these costs will be saved until the respective management applications are more closely examined later in the chapter.

Is This Application Cost Effective?

The least complicated version of cost effectiveness means getting the same effectiveness at less cost, or getting greater effectiveness at the same cost. In education, this translates to improving learning with no increase in cost, or reducing cost without adversely affecting learning. A more complex definition of cost effectiveness states that the benefits from increased effectiveness outweigh the drawbacks of higher costs. Unfortunately, we have no formula to measure any of these versions of cost effectiveness. It's difficult enough to reach agreement on acceptable measures of effectiveness. To complicate matters, it's virtually impossible to hang a price tag on increased knowledge; that is, how much more are we willing to pay to raise student achievement? Since we can't turn exclusively to hard data such as dollars and cents measured against test scores for answers, we need to combine whatever hard data we *do* have with our professional judgment, leading us to a calculated decision about the cost effectiveness of each use of computer technology.

With this overview of the criteria used to help us choose among various computer applications, we now put them to work as we return to each computer use discussed in earlier chapters.

CAL REVISITED: TAKING A HARD LOOK AT COMPUTER AS TEACHER

Computer Assisted Learning (CAL) continues to be one of the most dominant applications of computer technology in the schools. Is this because of its superiority compared to other uses, or is it because CAL is easy for teachers to implement? This section takes you through a series of questions to help you arrive at your own conclusions.

What Is the Rationale for CAL?

As shown in Chapter 2, the purpose of instruction can be grouped into three broad categories:

- understanding new material
- reviewing material already taught
- applying learned material to problems, situations, etc.

Within each category, you can identify suitable uses for CAL. If, for instance, your purpose is to have students understand new material, the tutorial mode of CAL is certainly appropriate. Serving as teacher, the computer engages the student in dialog and takes him or her through a lesson. This frees the teacher to concentrate on other students needing more personal attention. In a similar vein, the computer can be valuable if the instructional purpose is to review material already taught. Drill and practice are the most frequent uses of the computer as teacher. With its patient, non-judgmental style, the computer can help the student as long as the student chooses to engage in the instructional dialog. When the teacher's purpose is to apply material learned to new situations, computer simulation is particularly helpful, guiding the student through worlds he or she couldn't easily experience first hand.

So the question is not whether computers exist to help with instructional tasks. The question is more pointed: Does CAL adequately meet teachers' needs? To effectively answer this question, teachers need more than a casual acquaintance with CAL. They need a thorough understanding of specific computer programs designed to help teach specific topics. The decision-making process is somewhat analogous to selecting a student teacher. Not all teachers want student teachers all of the time. In fact, quite a few teachers don't feel a need for their services at all. Others choose to have student teachers based on certain instructional needs (plus a professional commitment to teacher education). But not just any student teacher will be acceptable. The teacher, ideally, makes a selection based on certain needs, including mutual agreement on teaching philosophy and techniques. Similarly, the teacher should screen CAL applications to make sure that the intended use matches the teacher's instructional needs at the moment; this includes compatibility on both philosophical and practical levels.

In summary, then, a rationale for CAL hinges on the individual teacher's assessment of CAL's appropriateness in the classroom. But this assessment requires actual hands-on experience with CAL programs to decide which, if any, can be used effectively to help carry out the various purposes of instruction identified earlier.

Where Can CAL Be Used Most Effectively?

Once everyone from the kindergarten teacher to the industrial education teacher at the high school discovers convincing reasons why CAL belongs in their domain, a tough decision must be faced. Who gets a piece of the action, and on what basis?

Assuming you aren't "flush with funds," scarce resources force a decision that not everyone gets computers for CAL. But who does get them? Are certain grade levels more entitled to this computer application? Does this type of computer use favor certain subject areas over others? Do specific groups of students such as gifted and talented, physically handicapped, and learning disabled students have a greater demonstrated need?

From a district perspective, the decision is particularly difficult because comparing needs of such disparate groups is like comparing apples and oranges. Not enough common attributes exist among the areas to arrive at an undisputable conclusion. One possible way out of this dilemma is to defer to research. Several studies have been conducted over a period of years, with mixed results. According to a current review of this research, the following factors are noteworthy regarding CAL effectiveness (Forman, 1981):

- The use of CAI (CAL) either improved or showed no difference when compared to traditional classroom approaches.

- When CAI and traditional instruction are compared, equal or better achievement is obtained with CAI, and in less time.

- Students have a positive attitude towards CAI, frequently accompanied by increased motivation, attention span, and attendance.

- Tutorial and drill modes seem to be more effective for low-ability students than for middle- or high-ability students.

- Many reluctant learners become active and interested when involved in computer-supported programs.

- The bulk of the studies showing CAI to be effective have concerned the use of adjunct CAI, in which the classroom teacher was readily available.

- Poor attitudes on the part of instructors and administrators have resulted in the overt sabotaging of the computer learning process.

- Foreign languages and science are two areas in which CAI programs consistently have proven effective.

- CAI is helpful to students reviewing materials with which they had prior familiarity.
- Retention rates may be lower over time than for traditional means.

More than likely, most districts won't be willing to hang their decision exclusively on an author's review of the research. Another factor that should weigh heavily in such a decision is the quality of the software, or computer programs, available for the application under consideration. Recall that the effectiveness of CAL rests largely with the strength of the computer programs designed to do the teaching. You may find, for instance, that certain subject areas have a bank of quality software, while other areas are virtually bankrupt of educationally sound programs.

Another factor to consider, in answering the effectiveness question, pits person against machine. That is, are there some CAL applications which can't effectively be duplicated by teachers? For example, if the purpose of instruction is to apply knowledge by simulating a crisis at a nuclear power plant, you may find that a teacher with excellent print materials can't match the computer's ability to combine sound, graphics, and motion, realistically creating the crisis and the student's role in it. Or, imagine a situation in which the computer with special devices allows a severely physically handicapped student to engage in a teacher-student dialog not available with conventional teaching methods.

Short of attempting to be egalitarian by letting all teachers take turns with the computers, you will be faced with deciding which teachers have the greatest need for computer assisted learning. The above considerations offer a starting point in your attempt to decide where computers can most effectively be used for CAL.

What Are the Costs Associated with CAL?

Keeping in mind the assumptions about costs outlined earlier in the chapter, let's study the total equipment costs for a hypothetical application at St. Theresa Middle School. Even though this example may not resemble your circumstances, at least the process used will show you how you can approximate the costs involved in implementing computer assisted learning.

Number of Hours Available Annually for Computer Use. Suppose St. Theresa has a six-hour school day and students attend school 180 days per year. The staff estimates that the computer actually will be turned on for about 70 percent of the available time. Seventy percent of the potential 1080 hours per year leaves 756 hours available for computer use.

Student Population Served. St. Theresa plans to serve the entire student body, or about 756 students, with its CAL applications.

Students per Computer. Recognizing that this figure fluctuates with the particular type of CAL computer program being used, the principal and teachers at St. Theresa agree that an average of two students at a time will use each computer.

Hours Available Annually for Each Student. Entering the above figures in the equation, the St. Theresa staff calculates the total hours per year that each student gets on the computer (see Figure 6-2). With an average of two students per computer, each student at St. Theresa gets two hours of computer time per year. To say it differently, if the St. Theresa school has one computer, given the other assumptions, each pupil can plan on interacting with the computer for two hours during the school year.

FIGURE 6-2. CALCULATING STUDENT COMPUTER TIME FOR ST. THERESA MIDDLE SCHOOL

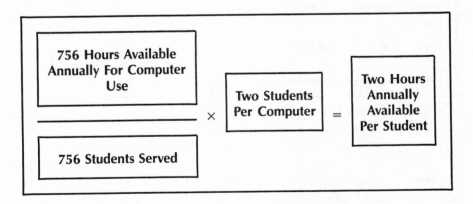

To apply rough cost estimates to this example, St. Theresa Middle School can buy two hours per year of computer time, per student, for $2,000—half representing the computer cost and half being the inevitable cost of software, maintenance, repair, and staff development.

Another way the St. Theresa staff can view costs is to decide how much annual computer time each student needs to achieve the curriculum goals. For Computer Assisted Learning, they can estimate how much time students should interact with the computer yearly in order to benefit from this learning medium. Suppose they decide that each student at St. Theresa should get one hour per week for 36 weeks, or 36 hours annually, on the computer for CAL purposes. Applying a derivative of the formula used earlier, the staff finds they can serve 42 students with one computer. Figure 6-3 outlines the steps in this calculation. If they want all students to use the computer an hour a week, they will need 18 computers (756 students divided by 42 students per computer).

**FIGURE 6-3. FORMULA FOR CALCULATING STUDENTS
SERVED PER COMPUTER**

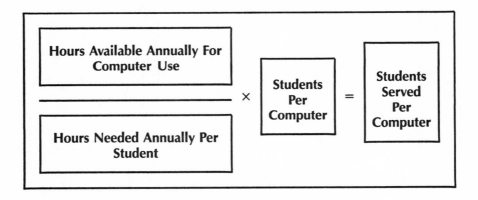

Returning to the question of costs, at a total price tag of $2,000 per computer application, 18 machines will cost St. Theresa $36,000. Keep in mind this figure is just for their school. You can continue the scenario by adding St. Theresa's figure of $36,000 to the costs calculated by other schools in the district.

Although the example just used was for an entire school, it's possible to implement CAL on a smaller scale. An individual teacher could conceivably have a computer in the classroom full time, using it exclusively for Computer Assisted Learning. To arrive at costs for a situation like this one, just insert the appropriate figures in the formula.

Is CAL Cost Effective?

It was easier to define cost effectiveness than to say whether or not CAL is cost effective. Unless the implementation of CAL saves personnel costs by substituting the computer for the teacher, CAL will carry a price tag that raises the total budget. With added costs to deal with, you need some basis for demonstrating CAL effectiveness. More than likely you won't have the luxury of field testing CAL applications for effectiveness. Instead, a combination of knowing about the CAL uses you are considering, along with your professional judgment about what price you are willing to pay for this technology, will guide you to a decision point. You may find, for instance, that CAL is most cost effective when the computer can teach in areas that are difficult for teachers, such as special education and simulated worlds in science class. Any way you add the numbers, though, added effectiveness will probably coexist with added costs.

DECIDING IF A COMPUTER LITERACY CURRICULUM IS WORTH THE INVESTMENT

Some of the computer applications discussed in this chapter can be skipped over without serious program or political consequences. The same cannot be said for the topic of computer literacy. Sooner or later, probably sooner than later, an assortment of forces will demand to know what your school plans to do about the computer illiterates walking the halls. You need to be in a position, regarding your program and politically, to respond on whether the idea of a computer literacy curriculum is worth the investment. This section is designed to help you with your response.

What Is the Rationale for a Computer Literacy Curriculum?

The core issue, however framed, is why it's necessary for students to have some experience learning with and about computers. A standard reply is that students will enter an adult world heavily dependent on computer technology. In fact, a vast majority of jobs in the next two decades will require some expertise with computers. For this reason alone, schools should seriously consider a computer literacy curriculum. But there's a more immediate reason. Currently, students meet computers in a nonsystematic way. In dark corners of arcades, in homes where such an expense isn't prohibitive, and in volunteer computer clubs, boys and girls, most often boys, begin their relationship with a computer. If we leave computer literacy to a self-selection procedure, we run the risk of having huge gaps in literacy between males and females, haves and have-nots, urban and suburban schools. The social and educational potential for this inequity can be partially addressed through a planned computer literacy curriculum for all students.

The issue doesn't rest so much with stating sound reasons why students should be computer literate. As discussed in Chapter 3, a synthesis of the research and practice indicates that all students should:

- understand how computers work
- understand the role of computers in society
- know how to operate and program computers
- use computers as a tool to meet various needs

The showdown comes when you have to balance this rationale against other viable claims for school resources. It's incumbent, then, upon you to give careful attention to why computer literacy should be taught, usually at the expense of something else.

Where Can a Computer Literacy Program Be Most Effectively Implemented?

Once you arrive at a program rationale, you need to decide where this new program will be implemented. Should it be a separate program, or integrated into the regular curriculum and existing units? Even though these questions will be revisited in more detail during the curriculum development phase, a tentative, general answer is required at this stage in order to respond to the issues of costs and cost effectiveness.

With only a few computers to go around, some districts opt to concentrate their resources at the secondary level. They take the position that all students should leave high school with some degree of computer literacy. Other districts head in the opposite direction, putting computer technology primarily at the elementary and middle school levels. These districts argue that children need exposure to computers early in their schooling to help ensure interest later on. Drawing from the research in mathematics, as well as evidence from attendance in computer classes and clubs, some educators claim that girls in particular need computer-related experiences in elementary school. By middle school, girls without these experiences shy away from participation in computer clubs and don't take the computer electives.

The effectiveness question goes beyond which grade levels and subject areas benefit the most from computer technology. It's also directed at the most appropriate location for the computers. With only one or two computers, many schools locate the equipment in the library, feeling that this high-traffic area provides the easiest access for the largest number of students. Other schools contend that teaching computer literacy with very few computers can most effectively be accomplished in a computer lab where there is more control over who participates and who teaches. Another arrangement is the mobile laboratory, putting computers on carts and wheeling them to the classrooms.

What Are Your Costs for Implementing a Computer Curriculum?

Costs of implementation are directly related to your answer to the previous question. The best way to approximate costs is to use the formula applied earlier in the computer assisted learning example.

In tracing through an example, we need to make some further assumptions. Foremost, assume that the decisions are based on a planning model governed by needs, not a reactive model based on what you can buy cheaply and quickly. Second, assume that the computer curriculum in question is for Wingspread, a high school of 1,000 students, only 500 of whom will participate in the computer curriculum. Next, assume that, on the average, each student should have access to the computer for about 30 minutes per week, or about 18 hours a year. Assuming you can handle an average of two students on the computer at a time, and assuming you can expect 756 hours available annually for computer use at Wingspread High School, you are in a position to arrive at your computer needs. Plugging the figures into the formula shown in Figure 6-4, you conclude that you can serve 84 students with each computer. Dividing the 500 students served by the 84 students per computer, you find that you need six computers to meet your needs. Estimating $1,000 per computer, the computer curriculum calls for a $6,000 hardware budget, plus $6,000 for all of the other costs referred to earlier.

FIGURE 6-4. CALCULATING STUDENTS SERVED PER COMPUTER FOR WINGSPREAD HIGH SCHOOL

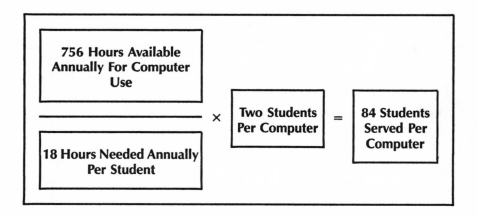

Now a serious issue arises if your budget can't accommodate these estimated computer costs. Do you modify your expectations by serving fewer students? Do you try to reduce time spent per student on the computer, which translates into reduced computer costs? If so, what impact does less computer time have on the curriculum expectations you originally had? It's quickly apparent how intricately the question of costs is tied to related curriculum questions. Regardless of how you ultimately resolve the costs issue, make your program decisions only after carefully considering the costs incurred. Using this strategy, you keep the integrity of your program by being realistic about what you can afford. All too often, we rush out and buy machines because the money is there, then we wonder what we can do with them. The results many times end up being either (a) computers inappropriately equipped for the needs we eventually identify, or (b) computer applications based on existing equipment, not on identified needs.

To summarize, arrive at your computer costs by first determining what kind of computer literacy curriculum needs you have. Next, make adjustments to costs according to a plan. These adjustments, usually in the form of reduced costs, should be reflected in computer curriculum changes. Attention to this issue will help prevent you from making promises on which you can't deliver, or asking for unrealistic budget amounts so you can uphold your promises.

Is Implementation of a Computer Literacy Curriculum Cost-Effective?

The answer to this question is bound up in the answers to other questions regarding a computer literacy curriculum. Diminished effectiveness is almost assured if you try to accomplish too much for the resources you have. In other words, it isn't cost effective to implement a program originally conceived at one budget level and currently operating at 60 percent of that budgeted amount. It also may not be cost effective to earmark large sums of money for a K-12 comprehensive computer literacy curriculum if other important areas of the curriculum suffer because of a large computer budget. Cost effectiveness can be achieved if careful planning of cost considerations is done before decisions about the scope of the computer curriculum are made, and if planners temper their visions of an ideal curriculum with what can be done effectively when competing with other priorities.

COMING TO GRIPS WITH CMI

In comparing the various computer applications for use in your school, management applications require the same serious scrutiny as instructional uses. In fact, decisions involving computer managed instruction assume added significance because of the wider audience affected. Specifically, any move to implement CMI generally means a move that affects the entire school, if not the whole district. It's difficult enough to introduce change into one teacher's classroom, which is possible with CAL, but to successfully implement a program across all grade levels or subjects calls for careful consideration of the issues involved. The following questions provide a framework for this consideration.

What Is the Rationale for Computer Managed Instruction?

Chapter 4 emphasized the point that CMI rested on three assumptions: mastery learning, individualized instruction, and teacher as instructional manager. CMI is not just a technology that can be tacked onto any instructional program. Philosophically, then, CMI carries an expectation that learning by objectives is a guiding influence in planning instruction. More than that, mastery of these objectives, defined as successful completion of the objectives according to some established criteria, is integral to a student's progressing through the curriculum. The curriculum, therefore, should be a clearly delineated path students follow as they master the objectives. In a similar way, the instructional process should be organized into a series of steps, usually along the lines of pretest, diagnosis, prescription, instruction, post-test, and diagnosis.

This view of curriculum and instruction supports the notion of individualization. Students should be able to move through their program at a pace and in a learning mode most appropriate for them as individuals. Conventional group-paced instruction doesn't meet the test of individualizing the curriculum. The assumption of teacher as instructional manager implies more than the teacher acting as clerk. It means that the teacher is responsible for using classroom data in managing the instructional decisions affecting each child. With an individualized program predicated on mastery learning, the volume of information to manage is much greater than the amount required when all students are at the same point at the same time.

With this brief review of the assumptions underlying CMI, you can quickly size up the immense effort needed to bring an entire staff around to this view of education, especially if they have spent many years teaching under a different set of assumptions. It's critical, then, to have your existing educational program compatible with the tenets of CMI before further considering computer technology for managing instruction.

Where Can CMI Be Used Most Effectively?

Deciding among grade levels and various subject areas can partly be eased by dealing with the previous question. Generally speaking, reading and mathematics have used CMI the most. A vast majority of these programs occur at the elementary level. A survey of the commercial CMI programs on the market verifies this finding. Usually CMI is implemented on a schoolwide basis. One reason for this goes back to the discussion of assumptions. To provide continuity and program coordination for students as they move through the grades, it is more likely that an entire school would adopt CMI, rather than just a few classes or grade levels. Also, it is financially advantageous to put the entire school's curriculum on a CMI system if the computer will be tied up with this application anyway.

The research evidence is sketchy regarding CMI effectiveness. Evaluation data from the Sherman School Project described in Chapter 4 yielded these findings (Chapin, 1977):

Individualization

- frees teachers of nearly all clerical tasks associated with individualization
- provides more instructional time
- reduces preparation time
- handles information faster than the manual system
- processes information faster
- costs compare to having an aide handle the clerical tasks of individualization

Attitudes

- teachers felt CMI was superior
- teachers supported CMI
- students preferred CMI
- parents misunderstood its functions

Achievement

- students do at least as well
- students use their time slightly more effectively

Somewhat offsetting these results were the conclusions reached in the evaluation of a two-year pilot test of the Wisconsin System for Instructional Management (WIS-SIM). The researchers found that, conceptually, computer managed instruction is sound. The evaluation failed to find, however, strong evidence that this system is cost effective in improving educational outcomes (Spuck et al., 1977).

Providing a final answer to the effectiveness question isn't easy. Once you determine which grade levels or subject areas are compatible with CMI, you probably have considerably narrowed those sites where CMI might be effective. Among these remaining options, you must next decide what CMI can contribute specifically to program goals in the various grade levels or subject areas under consideration.

What Are the Costs Associated with CMI?

After the effectiveness issue has been resolved, you should have a better idea of the factors influencing costs. As mentioned previously, a computer earmarked for CMI likely will not be used for any other application. Because of the time required to store and retrieve management information for the classroom teacher, you should figure costs on the assumption that the computer will be used exclusively for CMI.

Most of the early CMI systems operated on a time-sharing basis. Currently, however, CMI can be handled on a microcomputer system. According to reports based on the McFarland Project, a

$15,000 microcomputer, plus $2,000 per year operating costs, yielded a cost of $25,000 over a five-year period. This figure contrasts to the equivalent time-sharing system costs of $100,000 over five years (McIsaac and Baker, 1981). Systems recently have been designed that allow CMI to run on micros in the $3,000 price range. In addition, you need to consider peripherals like printers in your calculation of hardware costs. Assuming you decide to implement CMI in your school, and assuming you can get by with one micro for this purpose, the price tag for hardware could add up to a minimum of $3,000.

Closely related to hardware is software. It has proven an expensive venture for districts to hire personnel to develop software for their CMI. You could easily run up a bill of over $100,000 in software development costs alone. As curriculum modifications are made, the computer program has to be updated, again adding to the software costs. An alternative is to purchase your CMI program from a commercial publisher. Even this isn't cheap. What's more, generally you are bound by their curriculum, losing the flexibility of making curriculum changes in the CMI system as your staff desires.

An additional cost is salary paid to manage the abundant student information. To automate student data, the information must be entered into the computer. Usually, this must be entered via keyboard by a teacher or an aide. Depending on the scope of the CMI curriculum, a full-time aide could be required, at the very least. Clearly, personnel costs can quickly run up the total cost of a CMI system.

In adding up costs for a CMI project in your setting, keep several factors in mind. First, the machine probably will be used exclusively for CMI purposes. Second, the volume of data necessary to operate CMI means more memory requirements inside the computer than other computer applications, thus affecting the price of the computer. Along with the cost of the computer, determine necessary accessory equipment for implementing CMI. Third, get a realistic estimate of the costs involved in developing or buying software. Finally, take a hard look at the personnel costs associated with operating the CMI system. And don't forget to calculate the costs of equipment maintenance, repair, and staff development.

Is CMI Cost Effective?

Since the costs involved with CMI extend beyond those normally associated with classroom instruction, it's hard to deny that CMI is expensive. However, advocates of CMI quickly point out that the additional costs should be attributed to individualization, not computerization. That is, schools having an individualized program are more expensive to operate than those having a conventional program. An argument can even be presented that the extra personnel costs would be necessary to manage the instructional data generated by a manually managed curriculum that embraces individualization. At any rate, the costs outlined above still exist. Returning to the meaning of cost effectiveness, the idea of achieving the same results at less cost, or doing more with same cost is not possible under CMI. If CMI is to be sold on the basis of cost effectiveness, it's selling point is the belief that with added expense comes added effectiveness. Similarly, advocates of CMI might have a strong case in claiming that the additional costs are necessary to implement a program that complements the strongly held beliefs of staff and parents about how children learn best.

ANALYZING THE VALUE OF COMPUTERS
TO THE ADMINISTRATOR

Watching the rapid growth of computer technology in the offices of business and industry, it's safe to surmise that the field of education may move in that direction, too. As an aid to decision-making, you can use the questions listed below to help determine the value of computers to the school administrator.

What Is the Rationale for Computerizing
School Management Functions?

To answer this question, we turn again to the business sector. Executives point to time savings, money savings, and savings in human energy when a computerized management information system is installed. At a time when businesses are suffering through declines in revenue and profits, they still continue to expand investment in computerizing office procedures. In education, most school districts have used computer technology for a long time to help with their district-wide management functions. Now schools are wondering if they can likewise benefit from employing computers to act as administrative assistant. First, with personnel costs consuming about 80 percent of school budgets, any savings realized by a reduction in clerical salaries or by fewer requests for overtime and part-time help may provide substantial relief from budget pains. Second, computers can help save time. For many tasks, the computer can accomplish in seconds what takes hours for a secretary or principal. As described in Chapter 5, the creation and printing of reports can be handled quickly and accurately by computers. Also, if administrators can cut expenses in the form of saving human energy, this scarce energy can be spent more productively on the interpersonal interaction so important to a school setting.

Where Can a Computerized MIS Be Used Most Effectively?

With the librarian, guidance counselor, secretary, and principal each eyeing the computer as an opportunity to cut costs and time, some type of priority-setting must be done. Assuming an approximate cost of $3,000 per computer system for management tasks, more than one machine in a school could be difficult to justify. If you have only one computer for this purpose, perhaps the time can be allocated to meet various purposes. For example, in most schools, the secretary doesn't perform typing tasks more than 50 percent of the time. The other 50 percent of the computer's time could be used to produce the myriad of required reports by computerizing students files. Another option is to use this time to help manage educational tasks, such as scheduling classes and producing computerized report cards. Two things should be kept in mind, however, during the decision-making. First, make sure the application dictates the location, because once in place, the location will restrict the type of use the computer has. If the computer is in the secretary's office, chances are the machine won't be used to handle the librarian's administrative tasks or the guidance counselor's potential applications. Conversely, placing the computer in the library practically rules out using it for word processing activities in the office. A second point to keep in mind: Don't extend commitments for the computer's time unless you are confident the commitments can be met. Trying to use the computer in the office for word processing, scheduling, payroll, and student reports may result in none of the applications getting done with the quality or within the time frame you would like. It's politically more difficult but administratively more sound to decide on the most critical management needs to be met by the computer, and limit its use to those defined needs. This way you don't create false expectations from a variety of camps who will depend on the office computer to help with the work load.

Whatever direction you take, computerization of management tasks in the school will likely be a standard practice in the near future.

What Are Your Costs Associated with a Computerized MIS?

Just as in other computer uses, many expenses besides the purchase of the equipment cause administrators to really sharpen their pencils before making a commitment. A rough estimate of $3,000 per computer system was used earlier in discussing another management application, CMI. This amount actually includes an equipment package consisting of a 48K computer, monitor, at least one disk drive, and a quality printer. With equipment prices changing rapidly, any figure used will be obsolete soon. For discussion purposes, though, let's continue with $3,000 being the equipment cost. If every school in the district purchased one computer for management purposes, the total cost to the district mounts in a hurry. If a school buys the computer out of its own budget, the amount really leaves a dent in what's left for instructional purposes, particularly at the elementary level. In addition to the equipment purchase, you need to consider maintenance, repair, software, and staff development. Figuring another $3,000 over a three-year period (again an estimate) for these "hidden" costs, you face a budget request of $6,000. If you have 25 schools in your district, some budget or budgets would need to make room for $150,000 in additional expenses. Whatever the size of the district or school, a decision to computerize management functions necessarily means commitment to a considerable computer purchase.

Is a Computerized MIS Cost Effective?

Management tasks is one area in the "business" of education where some semblance of productivity can be measured. It's possible, for instance, on a pilot basis, to computerize a variety of school management functions in varied school settings. Efficiency is expressed in quantitative terms like time, money, and energy savings. With a controlled experiment similar to this sketchy outline, districts in fact could make cost effective decisions with solid data to support their recommendations. On a more limited scale, an individual school could do a study like this. If a study doesn't seem feasible, the sheer volume of information requiring management in the school, and the computer attributes of speed, accuracy, and reliability may be evidence enough to build a case for the computer's cost effectiveness in management functions.

DECIDING WHICH COMPUTER NEEDS
HAVE HIGHEST PRIORITY

A lot of the hard work is behind you after you have determined which computer applications are cost effective. At least you have narrowed the field for the next round of tough decisions. Specifically, you now need to decide which computer needs have the highest priority. Four steps, outlined below, are applied to the earlier example of the Wingspread High School.

Step One: Rank order the cost effective computer applications according to need. Unless you are in a rather unique position, you won't have enough resources to adequately implement every computer application on a broad scale. Therefore, limit your discussion to only cost effective use of the computer. Then, list in priority order the cost effective applications. Using the worksheet in Figure 6-5, Wingspread concluded that CAL, Computer Literacy, and a computerized MIS are the uses they can afford to consider at this time, with computer literacy being most important,

**FIGURE 6-5. COMPUTER APPLICATIONS
PRIORITY SETTING WORKSHEET
WINGSPREAD HIGH SCHOOL**

Computer Application	Cost Effective?	Rank Order	Equipment Needs	Equipment Costs	Other* Costs	Total Costs
Computer Assisted Learning	Yes	3	4	$4,000	$4,000	$ 8,000
Computer Literacy	Yes	1	6	$6,000	$6,000	$12,000
Computer Managed Instruction	No	—	—	—	—	—
Computerized Management Information System	Yes	2	1	$3,000	$3,000	$ 6,000
					Grand Total	$26,000

*Includes estimates of software, maintenance, staff development, and repair costs over a three-year period.

Budget Amount	$22,000

ADJUSTMENTS

Confine CAL to special education classes, saving $4,000 (2 computers at $1,000 each and $2,000 in other costs).

administrative uses second in importance, and CAL the least important among the cost effective applications.

Step Two: Calculate how much equipment is required to serve the students. With the instructional applications, CAL and computer literacy, you can use the formula described earlier to estimate computer costs. If you plan on implementing CMI or an MIS system, you have to estimate how many machines per school will be required to perform the necessary functions. In Wingspread's situation, they calculated that six machines met their computer literacy needs. An MIS system required one computer exclusively for that purpose. In addition, four computers were needed to implement CAL.

Step Three: Calculate the estimated price associated with decisions in Step Two. For purposes of this example, we'll assume that the computers will cost $1,000 each for both CAL and computer literacy, and $3,000 for an MIS. This translates to an equipment cost for Wingspread of $13,000, plus roughly $13,000 for all associated costs except personnel (see Figure 6-5 for a breakdown).

Step Four: Compare cost estimates to budget estimates and adjust where necessary. This step sometimes is painful to take. In the hypothetical case study, Wingspread decided that the budget simply can't accommodate nearly $26,000 worth of expenses for the three applications. To help in the decision-making, school officials asked some subsidiary questions:

- Do we fund all of Priority One before considering Priority Two?
- Can we reduce funding for a priority without jeopardizing the integrity of the project?

Both questions demand considerable attention. If, in fact, you have carefully considered your decision and concluded that computer literacy (in this case) is the first priority, and that it takes 12 computers to implement the computer literacy program, is it wise to cut back? If you cut back on your program to reduce equipment costs, undoubtedly your program won't be as strong as previously designed. If you cut back on equipment but try to maintain your program at the projected level, you again have put a dent in what you can do with fewer computers. On the other hand, if you ignore

CAL, a cost effective application you consider important, you are consciously acknowledging that you aren't going to fund a project you think is very important.

As difficult as the decision gets during this step, keep one thing in mind: You can't afford to jeopardize the integrity of any project just to add another one. That is, in trying to make room for as many priorities as possible, don't dilute your highest priorities to the point they are no longer effective. Following this advice, Wingspread decided (a) they needed all six computers to be effective in their computer literacy program, (b) the computerized MIS would be worth the investment, and (c) CAL would have to be pared back, implementing it only in special education classes, which required two computers to be effective.

Having plowed through the tedious, sometimes agonizing procedures discussed in this chapter, you should be in a position to begin shopping for computers. Chapter 7 guides you through the steps necessary to make the right hardware selection.

CHAPTER 6 REFERENCES

Botterell, A., "Why Johnny Can't Compute," *Microcomputing*, April 1982.

Chapin, J., *An Administrative Summary of the Madison Metropolitan School District's E.S.E.A. Title III Computer Managed Instruction Program: MICA*, Madison, WI, unpublished manuscript, 1977.

Eisele, J. E., "Instructional Computing: Using Computers in the Classroom: Look Before You Leap," *Educational Technology*, Nov. 1981.

Forman, D., *Instructional Use of Microcomputers: A Report on B.C.'s Pilot Project*, Province of British Columbia: Ministry of Education, 1981.

Gleason, G. T., "Microcomputers in Education: The State of the Art," *Educational Technology*, March 1981.

Luehrmann, A., "Planning for Computer Education—Problems and Opportunities for Administrators," *NASSP Bulletin*, April 1981.

McIsaac, D., and F. Baker, "Computer Managed Instruction System Implementation on a Microcomputer," *Educational Technology*, Oct. 1981.

O'Neil, H. F., Jr., ed., *Computer Based Instruction: A State of the Art Assessment*, New York: Academic Press, 1981.

Spuck, D., "An Analysis of the Cost-Effectiveness of CAI and Factors Associated with Its Successful Implementation," *AEDS Journal*, Fall 1981.

Spuck, D., et al., *Evaluation of the Wisconsin System for Instructional Management (WIS-SIM Pilot Test)*, Madison, WI: Wisconsin Research and Development Center, Technical Report No. 438, 1977.

Stewart, G., "How Should Schools Use Computers?" *Popular Computing*, Dec. 1981.

Thomas, J. L., ed., *Microcomputers in the Schools*, Phoenix, AZ: Oryx Press, 1981.

Young, G. P., "Electronics Technology for Public School Systems: A Superintendent's View," *Educational Technology*, Nov. 1981.

7

THE RIGHT WAY TO BUY A COMPUTER

When you made your last automobile purchase, did you begin by making a list of all manufacturers, noting base prices and costs for each option? Did you then construct a grid showing all these features, finally arriving at a decision based on the best buy from all of these data? Or were you like most of us in deciding on a car purchase? Did you decide on some essentials the car needed, talk with friends and recent purchasers, narrow the field to a handful of choices, then decide which car best met your needs at a price you could afford? As you've probably guessed by now, buying a computer system is much like buying an automobile. Both are major investments; both involve choice making from an endless array of companies, models, and options. The purpose of Chapter 7 is to help you wade through this morass of information and lead you to a rational decision regarding the purchase of a computer system. Following the guidelines offered in this chapter, you should be able to buy your computer system with confidence and a minimum of confusion.

FINALIZING YOUR COMPUTER TECHNOLOGY NEEDS

Once you work through the steps outlined in Chapter 6, you should have a grasp of which computer applications command priority attention in your setting. The basic question you have to ask is, "Do we really need computer technology to do what we want done?" It may be that you can find less expensive, more cost effective ways to achieve the same goal. If you've carefully followed the step-by-step approach outlined earlier and have decided that computer technology does indeed meet your needs, you're now ready to buy a computer system that fits these needs. Before proceeding, though, make sure commitment to the priority applications you've identified extends to those responsible for providing support, both financially and otherwise. Unless school district officials and the Board of Education agree with your decision on how to use computers in the schools, you may have some unpleasant surprises lurking ahead. Satisfied you have their support, you're ready to sally forth into the world of computer machines.

DECIDING ON THE TYPE OF
COMPUTER SYSTEM YOU NEED

Before turning to the particular features of a computer system, you must give some thought to the type of computer system you need. Most school districts employ one of the three basic types described below.

Time-Sharing Systems

Before the advent of the microcomputer, virtually all school district computer applications involved the time-sharing concept. To be more specific, "dumb" terminals were linked to a mainframe computer located at the central computing center of the district or another computer center such as a nearby university. The computer sent information along telephone lines to terminals in the participating schools. So a telephone hookup had to be installed at

for a computer in the school. Today, with
⸱ to schools wanting computer power, the
⸱aces stiff competition. The major advantage
bility to handle large volumes of data calling
apabilities. In addition, users have access to
programs stored in the main computer,
fely out of reach from possible damage by
ormer users of time-sharing report that the
⸱g drawbacks:

- The time-sharing system is slow; it doesn't process information very fast, and it can only handle one request at a time.
  Frequently you have to wait in line until you can get on line.

- Sometimes the system isn't available to users. Teachers
  report that the system seems to be down a lot, creating
  considerable inconvenience when the classroom teacher is
  all set to conduct a lesson. The down-time can be caused by
  the school's terminal equipment, the telephone company's
  equipment, or the mainframe computer.

- Time sharing is relatively expensive. Since costs are figured
  on a per unit rate, the more you use the system, the greater
  your total bill. Also, the rates are tied to the telephone
  company's pricing structure. Because more people want to
  use the system during conventional work hours, the per unit
  rate is higher during this period.

Microcomputer Systems

The disadvantages of time sharing turn out to be the strengths
of microcomputer systems. Specifically, micros offer the following
advantages.

- Micros are relatively inexpensive to operate. The McFarland
  CMI Project designers found that microcomputers saved the
  district approximately $20,000 per year over comparable use
  on time-sharing systems. In fact, unlike time-sharing, the
  more you use micros, the more inexpensive the unit operating cost becomes. Another cost savings occurs when adding
  peripherals. For instance, graphics, voice synthesis, and

music composition aren't considered practical to add to mainframe computers, but are available at reasonable costs for microcomputers.

- Microcomputers are reliable pieces of equipment. For the most part, schools report very little trouble with computer breakdown. When the machine acts "funny," simply restarting the program will often remedy the problem. When the computer does malfunction, the vendor likely will give you a loaner during the repair period.

- Micros are flexible systems. They are ready and waiting at any time during the day. They can even be taken home or transferred to other locations without worrying about the availability of a telephone hookup.

The only serious drawbacks to microcomputers are their limited ability to handle massive chunks of data and the need to have duplicate software for every micro used alone.

Networking Systems

The problem of duplicate software for each microcomputer in use is being solved by networking systems. In this type of arrangement, all of the microcomputers in a room share a common disk storage device for loading programs into the micros, but revert to their independent status when programs are loaded. Networking offers the following advantages (Wagner, 1981):

- The school doesn't have to buy separate disk drive or cassette recorders for each computer. The task is handled by a central storage and loading device.

- Software expense is minimized. Only one copy of the computer program is necessary, and teachers don't have to create a lot of backup copies of class disks.

The major disadvantage is the cost of the disk-sharing device. The most basic no-frill systems cost approximately $500. Higher quality systems cost several thousand dollars. To determine cost effectiveness, decide how many stations (microcomputers) will be available. By calculating how many disk drives you can eliminate, along with reduced costs for software and maintenance on the individual units, you should be in a position to decide if networking is a system your school should consider.

Whatever system you ultimately choose, make sure you carefully examine the features described in the next section.

FEATURES YOU SHOULD LOOK FOR IN EVERY COMPUTER SYSTEM

Returning to the car example, some items are essential regardless of which automobile you purchase. You're interested in gas mileage, ease of driving, durability, reliability, and price, among other features. The same is true of computer systems. Certain features are critical, regardless of what applications you have planned. This section highlights some essential characteristics to check out before you buy. You should feel free to modify this list as your circumstances dictate.

Software Selection

It's impossible to talk about buying a computer without becoming wrapped up in a discussion of software. Some computer educators would argue that decisions about software should be made before initiating talks about hardware. Actually, software and hardware decision making usually proceed together. Therefore, even though this chapter is Chapter 7 and the software discussion is found in Chapter 8, you should definitely read both chapters before acting on decisions about hardware or software. Anyway, the point to be made here is that the availability of quality software is basic to your equipment purchase. In fact, as stated earlier in the book, computer power is controlled only by the capabilities (such as memory) of the machine and the computer programs, or software, available to give the computer instructions. So the quantity and quality of software needed to carry out your computer applications should be a major influence in your hardware decisions.

Ease of Use

This general category can be narrowed according to your specifications. Essentially, a computer is easy to use if it requires a minimum of technical skill to operate, contains a keyboard format compatible with kids' needs, and has the flexibility to add devices such as joysticks, light pens, and printers.

Durability

Without question, a computer in school needs to withstand rugged use. Most students (and staff) don't intentionally abuse equipment, but the sheer numbers of people who daily move, set up, take down, operate, and occasionally bump or drop the equipment is justification enough to insist on durable hardware. By asking current users, discussing this issue with vendors, and reading trade magazine evaluations, you can sift through the maze of models to find which are most durable.

Reliability

With an investment of the magnitude that computer equipment requires, no school district can afford to have the hardware sitting in the shop while the computer application in the school goes unattended. Because so many firms are breaking into the computer market and new breakthroughs in technology are springing up at record pace, quality control is a serious problem. Just like in the car-building business, the introduction of something new in computer machinery carries with it the risk of "bugs" that need to be corrected. Some people avidly stay away from cars with new, "improved" features until these have proven reliable through extended use by the first customers to try them. The same rule applies to computers. Make sure your computer selection is backed by a proven record of reliability. This record can be uncovered through the same procedures you use to determine durability. Also, you can generally count on the firms that dominate the educational market to produce reliable products, at least those products that have been used in schools for some time.

Documentation

Documentation is computer jargon for the manuals, teacher guides, and other material explaining how to use the equipment. Considerable variability exists among manufacturers in their attempts to write material that is free of technical terms and rich with understandable teacher-oriented ideas. Imagine how the excitement of a new computer can be dampened when the teacher confronts these initial instructions in the user's manual:

> Welcome to your new computer. Before you get started, you should understand these things about your computer. It generates and uses radio frequency energy. It has been tested according to regulations for a Class B computing device, in accordance with the specifications in Subpart J of Part 15 of FCC rules. The main circuit of the computer is a Synertek/ MOS 6502 microprocessor, which runs at a rate of 1 million machine cycles per second and has an addressing range of 65,000 eight-bit bytes. Its repertory includes 50 instructions and 12 addressing modes.

The preceding information may be important to someone. But it's not what the first-time user wants to hear or read. You can save yourself a lot of agony, and probably expense, by selecting a computer system that recognizes your needs and reflects them in the way the support material for the machine is written. This documentation will be distributed widely to all teachers using the equipment. It should be self-explanatory so the computer specialists in the district aren't spending their valuable time interpreting jargon.

Expandability

Several theories are floating around about how expandable your computer system should be. In one camp are those who say you should buy the minimum system possible for the price you can afford and the needs you identify. When you outgrow the system, sell it or redirect its use to others who have these minimum needs, freeing you to buy a larger system. At the other extreme is a group who contends that you should initially buy as much capability as you can squeeze into your budget, even if you don't plan on tapping all of this capability in the near future. The reason behind this argument is that it's cheaper to buy the extra capability with the computer purchase than it is to add it later. A third group, camped somewhere in the middle, claims you should purchase a system that meets your current needs and those you expect to have in the near future, with an eye toward expansion as your needs change. In other words, the capability of expansion is what's important in their view (and probably the view shared by most experienced computer users). As you evaluate the various systems for expansion, don't narrow your focus to just memory expansion. Broaden your field to consider items like printers, scanners, and monitors. For example, some computer models can only accept a TV hookup, ruling out the use of a monitor. In summary, if what you see is what you get, and all you can get, is that what you want? If not, what expansion features are important for the computer application you have in mind?

Price

The price tag affixed to computers should be viewed with the same healthy skepticism as in looking at car prices. Price should be read as list price and, usually, base price. Competition is so keen in the computer market that the quoted price doesn't always mean the price you have to pay. As discussed in a later section, you can shop the various sources for computers and find considerable differences in price for the same unit. Also, this unit price generally reflects the cost of the computer without many, if any, options. The total price climbs well above the base price, depending on the options you choose to include in the package. Like car prices, though, some computer price tags include a few features as standard and other features at an additional cost. Another computer will package the features in a different way, making cost comparisons difficult at best. To complicate matters, you can't even get some features as an option, depending on the computer under consideration.

So, another caution to the prospective computer buyer: Don't be misled by the stated price. Check thoroughly to see what features are included for the money, and what the actual costs are.

When you feel confident you have an understanding of actual costs, cost comparison across brands is essential. Once you have comparison figures to work with, money will play an important role in your decision. But as in other major purchases you make, don't let the tail wag the dog. Don't let price dictate the brand you buy, because the cheapest isn't always the best. If the prices of comparable models are within 20 percent of each other, then other characteristics you evaluate should play a prominent role in your decision. Clearly, though, price is a major factor when you set out to buy equipment. Following the guidelines just mentioned, you should be in a better position to arrive at true costs and put them in appropriate perspective.

OPTIONAL FEATURES TO CONSIDER

After evaluating those features essential to any computer system, you need to examine other features essential for your particular application. Many of these characteristics are discussed below. Other specialized features you need more information about can be discussed with your computer dealer and studied in the computer journals.

Color

Before you decide that color computers are like color TVs— everybody should have at least one—examine carefully your intended computer application. Obviously, you pay extra to have color capabilities built into the computer, and color monitors also cost more. Unless your needs call for color in the video output, you can save money without sacrificing function by using either black and white or phosphorus-type displays. For instance, if your computer is targeted for administrative use, computer-managed instruction or word processing, color features serve very little purpose. The cost of buying color could be applied to purchasing a better quality printer, an item much more critical to your administrative needs. On the other hand, if you plan on using the computer to introduce young children to the world of computer technology, color plays an important role in motivation, as well as in teaching them how to tell the computer what to do.

In addition, some computer-as-teacher exercises at the high school level rely heavily on color to amplify, illustrate, and contrast various points in the lesson. A lot of the teaching power in these cases is lost when the lesson appears in black and white. Before you size up the color performance of various computers, size up your needs for color capability.

Graphics

It's difficult to engage in an extended discussion of graphics without getting mired down in technical terminology. For your purpose, you need to know if your computer application calls for graphics capabilities; if so, then someone needs to evaluate the quality of the graphics available. This quality spectrum is large, and adequate evaluation demands a knowledge of low-resolution and high-resolution graphics, along with the ability to interpret figures representing the individual blocks available for displaying graphics information. Generally speaking, the more blocks that can be displayed, the better the quality of the graphics. Before you're too deep in the mire, an extended discussion of this topic should be saved for a time when you need to know more about graphics and when someone with expertise can guide you through the discussion. For now, it's enough to know that if the use of graphics is important to your needs, you should pick your way carefully through the technical data because the graphics quality varies among the computers on the market.

Upper and Lower Case

Some people new to the computer field assume all computers produce output, just like typewriters, in upper- and lower-case letters. Not so. Several computers only have the capability to produce upper-case letters, while other computers offer lower case at extra cost. If you primarily want a display that's legible to the user, upper case works fine. If you need to produce reports, or if students will use the computer to write their compositions, you'll want the capability of lower-case letters, even if it costs a little more.

Available Languages

Despite the widespread popularity of BASIC as king of educational computer languages, its reign isn't absolute. With new developments in computer technology, other languages are gaining in popularity, particularly those suited for specialized uses. Numerous computers can accommodate only BASIC, and there are many versions of BASIC. Find out if your computer application requires a particular type of BASIC; if your needs are better met with another language, then double check the computers you are seriously considering to see if they can accept the language you need. As an illustration, suppose your primary purpose in having a computer is to write and implement computerized lessons for your class. Several newer languages, categorized as author languages, help you with this task by asking you a series of questions; you only need to supply the responses. Programming skills are kept to a minimum. If this kind of language meets your needs, you should select a computer that can accommodate the language. If, however, BASIC can satisfy your needs, you shouldn't pay a premium for the capability to run other languages for which you have little use.

Computer Memory

All computers require storage space inside them, and must hook up to devices that store information outside the computer. The more internal storage space available, usually the greater the cost. The message is simple: don't pay for storage space you don't think you'll need. This point was briefly covered in the discussion on expandability. To elaborate, the major storage space inside the computer you need to consider is called random access memory

(RAM). This is the amount of space available to you for loading programs and putting information into the computer. Some computer applications, such as simple programming, require as little as 1K or 2K of memory storage. However, programming in some of the more sophisticated languages requires a minimum of 64K. Many computers simply aren't designed to accommodate that much memory. To purchase a computer with 16K of RAM in order to run a program requiring 64K would be like buying a rowboat for water skiing. It won't work. So even if you have to summon all of the resource help possible, make sure you have a clear understanding of how much information storage is required for your computer application, and how much information storage each computer under consideration can handle.

Input and Output Capabilities

Each computer has some way to get information into and out of the computer in display form. Excluding very specialized applications, your computer will come with a keyboard input device and a monitor as the display device. With added cost, you can add other input and output capabilities. For instance, do you want joysticks, paddles, light pens, graphics tablets, or other devices to transfer information into the computer? Do you need printers, plotters, or other means for displaying data? By having a firm grasp on what you need to reach your computer application goals, you can decide if you need to look beyond the standard input and output devices in selecting your computer system.

The previously mentioned features are some of the more common options that potential computer users examine as they make their equipment decisions. Don't let this list blind you to the other characteristics you must add to your personalized checklist. And feel free to delete any of the items just discussed that don't pertain to your situation. In the end, though, you should have a specified list of features you apply to each computer under consideration. In the next section, you'll see how you can turn these characteristics into a worksheet for decision-making. Absent from this discussion has been a list of highly technical features found on many computers. If you are concerned about such items as the type of microprocessor used, the minimum and maximum RAM, the speed of execution, and the systems software available, you should consult a technical expert for advice. Another option is to combine your checklist with a checklist of technical features to arrive at a composite evaluation of the computer systems.

DEVELOPING A COMPUTER SELECTION CHECKLIST

Once you have decided on the features you want to include in your computer selection, you can transform this information into a checklist. Outlined below is a step-by-step process for developing and using such a checklist.

Step One: Decide which features are important to your application. As discussed previously, each application needs certain required capabilities. If particular brands of computers don't offer this capability, they should automatically be excluded from your shopping list. Other features, although not critical, will have some degree of importance to your application.

Step Two: For all of the features in Step One, you can assign a relative weight indicating how important each feature is for your needs. If all features are equally important, you can omit a weighting scale.

Step Three: Develop a rating scale that allows you to assign a qualitative value to each feature on the checklist. Mathematically, it works better to have the rating scale designed so that the highest number reflects the highest quality, down to the lowest number representing the lowest quality. An example of such a scale would be: 3 = strong, 2 = so-so, 1 = not so hot.

Step Four: Evaluate each feature according to the rating scale you developed.

Step Five: For each feature, multiply the weighted value by the assigned rating to arrive at a score.

Step Six: Add the score for each feature to get a total score for the computer being evaluated.

Step Seven: Compare total scores to determine which computers appear to best meet your needs. Small differences in scores should be disregarded since the evaluation checklist is only a

FIGURE 7-1. COMPUTER SELECTION CHECKLIST

CRITERIA	WEIGHT	RATING (Brands) A B C	SCORE A B C
Software Selection	3	1 2 3	3 6 9
Ease of Use	3	2 3 3	6 9 9
Durability	3	2 3 3	6 9 9
Reliability	3	1 3 2	3 9 6
Documentation	3	1 3 3	3 9 9
Expandability	2	2 2 2	4 4 4
Color	1	3 2 2	3 2 2
Graphics	1	1 2 2	1 2 2
Upper/Lower Case	2	2 2 2	4 4 4
Computer Memory	2	1 3 2	2 6 4
Input/Output Capabilities	2	1 3 3	2 6 6
TOTAL SCORE			37 66 64

WEIGHT	RATING
3 = critical	3 = strong
2 = important	2 = so-so
1 = not very important	1 = not so hot

rough guide to decision-making. It should not be construed as a precision instrument that strictly determines your selection.

Step Eight: Compare the handful of computers receiving the highest scores against the price of each unit to see which one would be the most cost effective. Be sure to include the cost of any optional equipment in the total price of each unit. *Caution:* be sure to double check that all finalists in the selection process have every characteristic you feel is critical to your computer application.

Step Nine: Prepare a set of hardware recommendations, including all of the information you have gathered in this step-by-step process.

In Figure 7-1, this process is applied to the hypothetical evaluation of three brands of computers, noncreatively labeled Brand A, Brand B, and Brand C. Note that Brands B and C are comparable in their total score and have all of the required features, and that Brand C is significantly less expensive. With this information, it is a rather straightforward process to develop recommendations supporting the purchase of Brand C.

SHOPPING FOR THE COMPUTER

When it's time to buy the computer, two questions need answers: Who decides on the purchase recommendations, and where should the computer be purchased? Let's look at each of these questions in turn.

Sometimes the person or group making the recommendation for a computer purchase also makes the decision. That's not always the case, however. The decision-making power falls into four broad categories. Ideally, those using the computer for a particular application should be the group making the recommendations, and ultimately, the decision. In reality, the decision often shifts to a higher level, especially if a large purchase is made. As an example, suppose all schools in a district evaluated which computer equipment to use in a computer literacy curriculum. The chances are high that the evaluations would be consolidated to produce a final set of recommendations. Based on this information, school district officials would make a bulk purchase of the same brand for all schools involved in the computer literacy curriculum. A third category of decison-making is the bidding process. That is, users of the application specify their needs, which in turn get translated into a bid specification. The company submitting the lowest bid gets the contract with the district. Particularly with technology like computer equipment, the bid process can be somewhat risky. To avoid buying computers that can't do everything you need, the school district must pay special attention that all specifications are clearly spelled out. In some cases, the bid process is controlled by writing the specifications so that only one vendor qualifies. A final way to arrive at computer decisions is to combine buying power into a consortium purchase. By several school districts agreeing to make a large-scale purchase, this consortium arrangement can supply adequate leverage to reduce costs far below what an individual school or district would have to pay.

The second consideration before shopping is deciding where to shop. Vendors can be broken down into four general classifications, each with its advantages and disadvantages.

Computer stores have been popping up everywhere, but most recently quite a few have faded quietly away. A major reason for this failure is the fierce price competition the computer stores face from other vendors. Because these stores offer only computer technology as their product, they need to operate with a higher profit margin than other sellers. Price, then, ends up being their biggest drawback. Another disadvantage is that most local stores sell only a limited number of brands, so their sales pitch is slanted toward just the few models they stock. Some buyers even report that the dealer gave them inaccurate information, which they discovered as they tried to get the computer to live up to the promises it couldn't keep. On the positive side, computer stores have the advantage of being local. When service is required, they are as close as your nearest phone. This feature proves particularly useful when your entire computer curriculum or other application depends on having computer equipment that always works. Many times the local dealer will supply you with a loaner while your equipment is being repaired. Service should be a major factor as you decide where to shop.

As the computer equipment business continues to grow, a larger number of retail department stores are getting into the act. Because computer sales are just a sideline with these retailers, they tend to be very price-competitive. Herein lies their major advantage. The biggest disadvantage is the lack of service. Most retailers don't employ trained technicians to handle computer equipment problems. Taking your broken computer to the local computer store, after buying it from another source, isn't likely to gain you much favor in the eyes of the store personnel. Some stores even refuse to provide repair service on equipment unless it was purchased from them. Another disadvantage of department stores is the absence of trained salespeople. Most educators need a lot of assistance as they wade through all of the technical details. When the clerk responds with, "I'm not sure; I'll have to check with my boss when she returns," or "Let me see if the manual answers your question," you become a little apprehensive about whatever advice the clerk does offer.

Many computers can be purchased at discount prices through mail-order outlets. Again, price is their drawing card. Their major drawback is lack of service. They can ask rock-bottom prices because they have very little overhead in the form of personnel. They don't have trained repair technicians; many times they don't even have knowledgeable salespeople who can answer your phone queries. Returning to the old saying, with most mail-order dealers, "What you see is what you get."

A limited number of manufacturers operate their own computer stores, selling directly to the consumer. This arrangement offers the advantage of having salespeople who are very informed about their products. Combining this knowledge base with the availability of local service and competitive prices ensured by eliminating the middleman, these vendors can effectively respond to a lot of school district needs—IF the district has clearly determined this manufacturer sells the best equipment for their needs. The big disadvantage is that you get a sales pitch for only one brand. If you need to compare several brands, you'll have to visit other stores.

As computers chart a reliable pattern of sales in the educational market, other creative ways will emerge to purchase computer equipment. For now, each type of vendor offers advantages and disadvantages you must weigh before you go computer shopping.

COMPLETING THE COMPUTER SYSTEM

The major emphasis of Chapter 7 has been on the purchase of the heart of the computer system, the computer itself. This unit is not only the heart, it's the brains of the system. Understandably, then, your final purchase decision is governed by your evaluation of the computer. However, as caricaturized in *The Wizard of Oz,* anything needs more than a heart and brain to function as a whole. The same is true with computers. To complete the system, you need at least an output device and an external storage device.

As discussed elsewhere in the book, the basic output device is the monitor. This display unit can range from an inexpensive old black and white TV to a relatively expensive computer monitor designed to display the color features of the computer. What you select depends on your needs. Make sure, however, you give due attention to the price and quality of the output devices you evaluate. Pay particular attention to whether the monitor is included as part of the system or treated as an option.

The final ingredient of a minimal computer system is the external storage device. The most popular types of equipment for educational applications are the cassette recorder and the disk drive. Their relative advantages and disadvantages have been highlighted in Chapter 1. The main distinctions between them are speed and cost. Many cassettes can be purchased for under $100, while disk drives can run several hundred dollars. If speed of transmitting information isn't critical, the cassette might be a cost effective route. If you need to store large amounts of information and speed is important to you, then a disk drive will probably be your best bet, even though it carries a higher price tag. When making cost comparisons, note that some companies build the disk drive into the computer housing. Therefore, the system price reflects the cost of the disk drive. Most companies have designed their disk drives as separate units and priced them accordingly. So, check to verify that your cost quotations accurately reflect total costs for the entire computer system, not just the computer itself.

This chapter has described the basic elements of a computer system you should consider as you begin your computer shopping, and has outlined a step-by-step model as your shopping guide. Your task is to turn this model into a powerful tool that enables you to make wise decisions when it comes to selecting your computer system. Before you make any final decisions, however, you should pay close attention to the points regarding software outlined in the next chapter.

CHAPTER 7 REFERENCES

Braun, L., "Help! What Computer Should I Buy?" *Mathematics Teacher*, Nov. 1981.

Brumbaugh, K., "Microcomputers vs. Time Sharing," *Creative Computing*, March 1981.

Finkel, L., "Buying a Micro: What Every Educator Should Know," *Electronic Learning*, Jan./Feb. 1982.

Segal, H., and J. Berst, *How to Select Your Small Computer ... Without Frustration*, Boulder, CO: Association of Computer Users, 1981.

Wagner, W., "Disk Sharing: The Best of Two Worlds," *Classroom Computer News*, May/June 1981.

Watt, D., "What Computer Should a School Buy?" *Popular Computing*, Dec. 1982.

8

FINDING
THE RIGHT SOFTWARE

Aside from the computer's capabilities, the single most powerful influence in shaping the success of your computer project is educational software. Therefore, once you sift through the piles of software and find those items most suitable for your use, you're ready to begin the project. But the sifting is not as simple as it may appear. Consider that the catalog of one large distributor provides descriptions of over 1,000 programs by 48 publishers. On top of all of these offerings, teachers, students, and sometimes parents add to the pile of software with their own creations. Some of these computer programs represent the highest quality work. Most, though, leave a lot to be desired. The purpose of Chapter 8 is to help you sort through the large volume of software and apply sound criteria as you consider those programs best suited to your needs.

THE HARDWARE-SOFTWARE CONNECTION

Feeling the pressures of time and money, many educators begin their computer project with an assortment of computer brands, each representing the best buy at the moment. After selecting the software most appropriate for their project, these enterprising individuals come face to face with the computer industry's nemesis: nonstandardization of software. To put it more plainly, computer programs you buy to run on one brand of machine won't run on other brands. In fact, you cannot even assume that the software you purchase will run on any other model of equipment by the same company. The caveat contained in this message is simple but significant: Look for the hardware-software connection. Don't buy equipment until you determine that the type of software application you want will run on the equipment you are considering, keeping in mind that different brands of equipment call for different versions of software.

IMPROVING THE QUALITY CONTROL OF SOFTWARE

Unlike the textbook publishing industry, the software industry presently crawls along, watching for hints that it should pick up the pace. Part of the foot-dragging stems from a nagging concern called the copyright problem. So far, the software publishers have failed to successfully prevent or discourage "copyright pirates" from illegally copying material. Many people simply don't admit that unauthorized duplication of software is stealing. Others admit it, but turn the copying into a profitable business by selling the pirated software for less than market value. All of these forces drain the potential software market, causing commercial publishers to view the market from a distance. They are unwilling to make a sizeable investment in an unpredictable market.

And software development is a sizeable investment. Depending on the sophistication of the product, commercial development expenses run between $2,000 to $5,000 for each minute of student contact time built into a software package. The industry estimate for minimum development time hovers around 100 hours. If you add the additional costs of writing documentation, field testing, and marketing the program, it's easy to see why publishers are reluctant to undertake such efforts when the return on their investment remains suspect. This posture sets in motion a circular reaction. Because many of the publishers refuse to jump into the software market, quality software is hard to find. Because of this condition, some potential purchasers of computers have abstained until quality software arrives. Without more people buying computers and, consequently, software, potential publishers continue to hold back. So it goes.

The software market suffers an additional loss as more school districts connect microcomputers via networks. By using the network concept, a school can purchase only one copy of a computer program because the master disk drive will load a classroom full of machines all at once. Networking introduces another copyright dilemma. Should a school district buy enough programs to match the number of machines in order to comply with copyright laws?

Contributing to the software quality control problem, the "electronic cottage industry" churns out software for sale. With profit as the prime motive, ambitious entrepreneurs develop anything the consumer will buy. Some of the most sophisticated software on the market originated in garages and basements of talented computer specialists. More typical, however, is an electronic cottage industry characterized by instability, resulting in disgruntled buyers and out-of-business sellers. This negative publicity damages the credibility of those who do work hard to produce quality software.

Even computer programmers with good intentions sometimes unwittingly have a negative effect on quality control because they have little, if any, experience in the field of education. Programs that are technically sound won't score very high if they don't reflect sound teaching principles. For example, a drill and practice program that fails to use appropriate reinforcement strategies, and ignores the fact that children need varying amounts of drill and different types of practice, probably won't last very long on the competitive market—lingering only long enough for teachers to form unfavorable opinions about the quality of software available.

Returning to the point established at the beginning of the chapter, it's no exaggeration that your computer becomes useless as a tool to assist learning if you **can't** find software that adequately fits your computer application **and** individual needs. To help you prevent this from happening, the balance of this chapter provides a step-by-step approach for locating and evaluating software.

LOCATING QUALITY SOFTWARE

As emphasized many times throughout this book, the educational needs of your classroom, school, or district should govern how you use computers. The same principle applies to the selection of software. As described in Chapter 2, there are three basic purposes of instruction that can be identified:

- understanding new material
- reviewing material already taught
- applying material learned to problems, issues, situations, etc.

Your software selection, therefore, should be geared toward meeting a specific purpose of instruction. But how do you begin this selection process?

The first step is to know the various sources for locating quality software. A logical starting point is to visit your local computer store. You should not anticipate, however, a smorgasbord of software on display. Because of the relatively small number of buyers shopping at computer stores for educational software, the vendor can't afford to stockpile a large inventory. Instead, the merchant will show you numerous catalogs and invite you to place an order. Most catalogs limit product information to a few sentences describing the contents of the software. It's unlikely you will have the chance to preview any of these materials because the vendor won't have them in stock. Further, many publishers don't encourage previewing due to the risks of illegal copying, and thus no sale.

Armed with this somewhat discouraging news, it's clear you need to do some homework in locating the software that best fits your needs. One of the most reliable sources of information regarding software is the informal network of friends and colleagues who have needs similar to yours. Talk with others who have implemented computer applications like the one you are planning. Find out what works and what doesn't work. In addition, ask about vendors who have a proven track record in meeting customers' needs.

Another source of software is the local computer users' groups. Most of the large computer manufacturers actively encourage participation in user groups by compiling a mailing list of buyers along with a description of how they are using computers in their setting. Even some of the more broadly focused user groups will have subgroups with a primary interest in educational applications. At group meetings and during informal sessions, group members enjoy swapping software.

This idea of software exchange has been institutionalized by the SOFTSWAP educational clearinghouse operated by the San Mateo, California Office of Education and the Computer Using Educators. They collect and disseminate uncopyrighted software for the brands of microcomputers most commonly used in schools. You can buy the disk of your choice for a nominal price (around $10), or you can receive a disk in exchange for each original program you contribute.

A growing number of educational service agencies collect samples of software for their constituents to preview. State departments of education, regional service agencies, individual school districts, and some university-affiliated research centers loan computer programs to schools for preview prior to purchase. Even if the service agencies charge a modest fee for participation in such a network, the schools will find this service a cost-effective way to locate quality software.

An often overlooked source of programs is computer magazines. Having educators as the primary audience, many of these journals make available excellent computer programs for the consumer to copy. Some teachers report success with having students first type these programs into the computer, then save them on cassette or disk for later use. This experience also helps students have a better understanding of how a program achieves specified results.

EVALUATING THE QUALITY OF SOFTWARE

Once you locate the sources of software for your computer application, you need some criteria for deciding on the relative worth of the mass of programs on the market. The purpose of this section is to guide you through the evaluation process by presenting criteria organized along three dimensions: technical quality, content quality, and instructional quality. These criteria have an instructional orientation, reflecting the dominant uses of computers in schools today. However, you can easily adapt the items to management applications if the need arises.

Technical Quality

Any time you buy textbooks for your classroom, you know with certainty the books will contain print and pictures, just like you ordered. Technically speaking, the books work. In the current world of educational software, you can't be so sure. The following questions help you assess the technical qualities of the software you are considering.

What Is the Quality of the Warranty?

Warranties for microcomputer software range from nonexistent to comprehensive. At the very least, you should look for a guarantee that the program is free of errors or "bugs." A program that won't function properly is worthless to the typical user who is untrained in locating and fixing errors. Some companies are willing to warrant their software free from bugs for a fixed period of time, say 90 days. Also, many companies will agree to sell at a discount revisions of software when you return the earlier version.

How Well Does the Program Run on Your Equipment?

As ridiculous as this may seem, you can buy programs to use in your classroom that simply won't run. Somewhat similar to the production of new models of an automobile, new models of software contain bugs that need to be corrected. In the case of cars, though, the vehicle usually will run even with the bug. Not true with computer programs. Many times, one seemingly little bug will render a lengthy computer program inoperable. As the software is revised and refined, a lot of these problems will disappear. However, for your own protection, make sure your new software runs on the computer you will be using.

How Easy Is the Program to Use?

The term "easy to use" takes on a rather comprehensive meaning when it refers to educational software. To begin with, the user should be able to operate the program independently, freeing the teacher to work with other students. This means the program's instructions must be clearly stated and written at a reading level for the targeted audience.

Another element affecting use is the keyboard skills required of the student. Particularly at the elementary level, children have insufficient dexterity to handle a lot of typing. Software packages having excellent instructional qualities may receive little attention because students become frustrated with the typing involved. Some developers try to get around the typing problem by using computer accessories such as light pens, joysticks, or game paddles to control the computer. In an era of tight budgets, though, these "luxuries" may be hard to justify. Programs that focus on thinking skills and minimize keyboarding will avoid this problem.

Finally, the program should be easy to terminate. Some otherwise strong programs lose appeal because students have to endure the entire program, even if they've finished their assignment. To put it in computer jargon, students need the option of "escaping" the program.

How Does the Program Handle Unexpected Responses?

While some computer software operates smoothly when predicted student responses occur, the program quits functioning properly, or "crashes," when the unexpected happens. To test the response flexibility of your software, work through the program being previewed at least three times. On the first trial, do everything the correct way—as your best student might. The second time through, play the role of the average student, making a few mistakes. Finally, respond as the student who is trying to "crash" the program. What happens when an unanticipated response is fed into the computer? For instance, does the computer request a numeral as a response but accepts a letter or other symbol? The best software developers anticipate a wide range of student responses and program accordingly.

What Is the Quality of Grammar and Spelling?

In contemporary software, it's common to find spelling and punctuation errors, as well as faulty sentence structure. Not only are such errors distracting, they are also bad instructional models for students. Furthermore, poor grammar and spelling often reflect on the skills and dedication of the software designer.

To What Extent Does the Student Control the Presentation of the Material?

Ideally, students should be able to set the pace of instruction commensurate with their individual reading speed. Some software, however, presents material at a uniform pace, ignoring the needs of the individual student.

Also, the ability to easily manipulate the program is important to students. More specifically, students should have the option of skipping the instructions and moving right into the dialog with the computer. They should also be able to advance to a particular point in the program, without having to witness a presentation of material they've already mastered.

How Appealing Is the Program?

For optimal use, the display should be uncluttered and easily readable. Too many programs are nothing more than books put on a computer screen. As pointed out in Chapter 1, graphics adds a special value dimension—if used appropriately. Sometimes, software designers get carried away with cute little figures fluttering across the screen, or happy faces smiling all over the place. Unnecessary noise can also be distracting. Repetitive "squirts," or the same musical measures played after every response get in the way of learning. On the other side of the picture, plenty of programs offer the consumer an excellent blend of text, sound, and graphics to create an appealing software package, a combination you should strive for as you evaluate software.

Content Quality

Even the most technically impeccable software should be scrapped if the quality of the content is inadequate. Following are some basic questions to guide your content evaluation.

Is the Content Educationally Important?

Undoubtedly much of the educational software on the market is not educational. It may be entertaining. It may be attention-getting. But it may not belong in a classroom. Just as you screen other instructional materials such as texts, films, and guest speakers, you need to apply the same rigorous evaluation to software.

Does the Content Match Your Existing Curriculum?

Frequently we run across interesting activities for students but we don't have the curriculum to match. When you find an interesting computer program that doesn't fit your curriculum, you have three options. First, you can decide the program is educationally valuable but not specifically relevant to your objectives and file it for future reference. Second, you can modify your curriculum to make room for the program that's too good to leave out of your teaching. For example, assume you've found an exciting software package that requires students to participate in a simulation about crop production and world hunger. Although world hunger is not part of your curriculum, perhaps you're so impressed by the "higher order" thinking skills, you decide to include the topic because of its emphasis on an important skill. Third, you can build a unit around the contents of the software you've found. This computer application could be the stimulus needed to launch an exciting new topic into your curriculum.

To What Extent Is the Content Factually Accurate?

Too frequently we purchase programs without adequate information about the expertise of the developers in the targeted subject area. By screening prior to purchase, you can avoid the chance of providing misinformation to students. In substantive areas such as social studies and science, it is particularly crucial to assure accurate content. Incorrect knowledge about the effects of combining chemicals could be dangerous!

How Appropriate Is the Content for Your Students?

As you evaluate software, keep in mind such variables as age, grade, and skill level of your students. Many software designers target the average child, and consequently miss the student who needs material at a different level. For example, the fifth-grade teacher of disadvantaged students can't rely on the publisher's claims of science software aimed at the fifth-grade level. An in-depth evaluation may show that the content is much too difficult for this particular class.

Instructional Quality

A high score on content quality does not necessarily mean that the software qualifies for inclusion in your curriculum. To teachers, another important dimension is instructional quality. The questions outlined below deserve scrutiny as you evaluate software.

How Appropriate Is the Computer for Your Activity?

Basic to any decision regarding the use of educational software is the appropriateness of the computer to your activity. Just because software titles correspond to your lesson doesn't automatically qualify them as effective educational tools. You may find that other instructional media and techniques achieve the same results more effectively. Some teachers claim, for instance, that the flash card method still is the best way to provide drill and practice in teaching multiplication facts. When you do conclude that the computer and accompanying software are appropriate for your purposes, you're ready to evaluate more carefully the instructional quality of the software.

How Well Does the Software Achieve Its Stated Goals?

Most teachers and administrators have learned the hard way that publishers don't always deliver on their promises about the content of the material they're selling. Typically, vendors of educational materials want to stretch their sales market to its outer limit, so they write glowing and expansive comments about the purpose, audience, and activities included in their software. You, however, end up with the responsibility of deciding if, indeed, the software achieves its stated goals. To make this decision, you need to make a careful comparison between the publisher's promises and the actual instructional material.

Ideally, the documentation will include evaluation data from the field testing of these programs. These results should provide such information as pre- and post-test scores to verify the promised gains in student achievement. Learning to read this type of research report gives additional ammunition in your task of selecting the very best instructional materials to meet your goals. In the absence of or in addition to such evidence, you ultimately hang the decision on your own professional judgment.

How Effective Is the Instructional Technique for Teaching Your Objectives?

Returning once again to the purposes of instruction, it's critical that the software you select matches your purpose for the lesson. As an illustration, introducing new information to students will not be done very effectively using drill and practice software. On the other hand, students ready to apply their knowledge will become quickly bored with too many tutorials on the same topic. As an illustration, complex issues surrounding a presidential campaign are likely to be better understood through a simulation than through didactic teaching.

How Effective Is the Feedback the Program Presents to Students?

For maximum effectiveness, the software should engage in ongoing dialog with students regarding their progress. A major part of this dialog includes immediate, appropriate feedback about performance. Ultimately, you must decide what qualifies as appropriate for your students. Some programs attempt to be humorous by responding sarcastically to student errors with such comments as, "No, dummy, that's wrong!" Most teachers find this type of response offensive and discouraging to students. A more sympathetic response might be something like, "Sorry, try again."

Feedback offered by the computer must also take into account the response pattern of the student. An early version of a program to teach students states and capitals gave students three opportunities to identify the correct answer, and if they were unsuccessful, the program moved to another question, never indicating the right choice. A program like this does not incorporate what we know about how students learn best.

In many of the early computer programs, each right answer led to a happy face or similar reward for the student. Now educators question the value of providing positive responses to students for every right answer. Some observe that students become bored with the happy face, and in fact resent the dead time before the computer moves to another activity. Another twist to this problem exists when software designers make the reinforcement to wrong answers more appealing than responses to correct answers. As developers become more sensitive to these concerns, you should see more judicious and effective use of reinforcement.

SIMPLE CHECKS FOR ASSESSING SOFTWARE

Now that you have a solid background regarding the elements comprising quality software, you can use the checklist shown in Figure 8-1 to evaluate the programs you consider purchasing. Although the points covered in the checklist represent the most common attributes to look for, you should modify the checklist to fit your particular needs.

FIGURE 8-1. SOFTWARE EVALUATION FORM

Program Title	Publisher/Author	Copyright
Computer Brand/Model	Minimum Computer Requirements (e.g., "K," cassette/disk, TV/monitor)	
Program Uses (e.g., drill, tutorial, testing)	Subject/Topic	

Criteria	Strong-Weak (5 4 3 2 1)	Comments
TECHNICAL QUALITY **Warranty**		
Software-Hardware Compatibility		
Ease of Use		
Flexibility in Response Patterns		
Grammar/Spelling		
Appeal-Interest		
CONTENT QUALITY **Educational Importance**		
Factual Accuracy		
Appropriateness for Students		
INSTRUCTIONAL QUALITY **Appropriateness of Computer as Medium of Instruction**		
Achievement of Stated Goals		
Effectiveness as Instructional Technique		
Effectiveness of Computer Feedback		

```
┌─────────────────────────────────────────────────────────┐
│  ┌──────────────────────────┐                            │
│  │ OVERALL RATING           │                            │
│  │   Strong-Weak            │                            │
│  │   ( 5 4 3 2 1 )          │                            │
│  └──────────────────────────┘                            │
│                             RECOMMEND                     │
│                                                           │
│         Yes, if _____  │
│            No _____  │
│                                                           │
│                                                           │
│       _____    _____   _____   │
│          Reviewer            School           Position    │
└─────────────────────────────────────────────────────────┘
```

In the last few years, another source of software evaluation has emerged. Clearinghouses have been organized to provide users with comprehensive reviews of software. Sometimes these firms operate as independent, profit-oriented businesses. Other clearinghouses operate as educational service agencies, with software evaluation as one of their primary services. Many times you can request software evaluation by a particular topic or subject area. Sometimes the clearinghouse charges a fee for these services.

Most of the educational computing journals have a department devoted to software review. Recently, one journal decided to focus exclusively on software evaluation. Even with these efforts, less than 5 percent of the available educational programs receive formal evaluation through this medium.

DEVELOPING YOUR OWN SOFTWARE

What if you can't find commercial software to meet your computing needs? An alternative course of action is to develop your own. Despite the temptation to argue that only you know the needs of your students, your curriculum, and the instructional techniques that work best in your classroom, you should heed the warnings of those who preceded you in developing software.

The first and loudest warning is about development costs. As mentioned earlier in the chapter, 100 hours seems to be an ultra-conservative estimate of time needed for software development. More than likely, you can double or triple this figure for anyone but the most experienced programmer. As a district, you must decide if these costs are worth the payoff of customized software for your particular application.

Another warning points to the need for a team approach to software development. Experience shows that a single person, working in isolation, can't develop quality software—particularly if this person has a full-time job unrelated to software design. If you convene a team to develop your computer programs, consider including a computer programmer, a specialist in learning, and an expert in the specific subject contained in the software.

As a final caveat for the do-it-yourself software developer, follow a set of guidelines similar to the points in the checklist. Any skilled designer needs a pattern. The checklist serves as a guide to help you shape the final product.

Whatever your final decision, whether you purchase software commercially or you develop your own, the quality of the product plays a critical role in the reception your computer receives. When we can boast of a broad repertoire of high-quality software, we can more assuredly forecast that computers will find a permanent place in our schools.

To pave the way for their entry, we also need a solid plan of action for moving from development to implementation. Chapter 9 takes you step by step through such a plan.

CHAPTER 8 REFERENCES

Hakansson, J., "How to Evaluate Educational Courseware," *The Journal of Courseware Review*, Sept. 1981.

Heck, W., J. Johnson, and R. Kansky, *Guidelines for Evaluating Computerized Instructional Materials*, Reston, VA: National Council of Teachers of Mathematics, 1981.

Kingman, J., "Designing Good Educational Software," *Creative Computing*, Oct. 1981.

Malone, T. W., *What Makes Things Fun to Learn? A Study of Intrinsically Motivating Computer Games*, Palo Alto, CA: Xerox Palo Alto Research Center, 1980.

MicroSIFT, *Evaluator's Guide for Microcomputer Based Instructional Packages*, Eugene, OR: International Council for Computers in Education, 1982.

Roblyer, M. D., "The Case For and Against Teacher-Developed Microcomputer Courseware," *Educational Technology*, Jan. 1983.

DEVELOPING AN ACTION PLAN FOR IMPLEMENTING COMPUTER TECHNOLOGY

Many times, old fairy tales have a way of softly sending a message containing a contemporary reality. In *Alice in Wonderland,* the Cheshire Cat and Alice hold a classic discussion paraphrased below (Carroll, 1960).

"Cheshire Puss, would you please tell me which way I ought to go from here?"
"That depends a good deal on where you want to get to," said the cat.
"I don't much care where I get to," said Alice.
"Then it doesn't matter which way you go," said the cat.
"Just so long as I get somewhere," Alice added as an explanation.
"Oh, you're sure to do that," said the cat, "if you only walk long enough."

In education, we've certainly walked long enough, retracing our steps countless times as we try to decide where we "ought to go from here." If we had heeded the advice of the Cheshire Cat and considered carefully a final destination, we might have gotten there sooner—those infrequent times we got there at all. Even couched in fairy tale language the message is clear: We should take stock of where we are going, because, unlike Alice, we do care where we end up.

All too frequently where we've landed is a dead-end street housing well-intended innovations in education. Teachers, administrators, and parents vividly recall the endless parade of attractions passing down the street. Trying to separate the parade winners from losers over the last half-century has left many educators tired and sighing, "This too shall pass." Most veterans in our schools don't need to read the research results to come to the same conclusion: A vast majority of so-called innovations were blunted on schoolhouse and classroom doors, never actually reaching the kids. But it's not too late to mend our ways; we can learn from our mistakes and improve the probability that our curriculum change efforts will penetrate the schoolhouse and classroom doors, ultimately making a difference in children's learning.

The general lessons learned from unsuccessful curriculum change can be applied to the specific case of introducing computer technology into the schools. The purpose of this chapter is to draw on both the past successes and failures to build a framework for change that increases your chances of effectively implementing computer technology in your setting. This doesn't mean you will leave Chapter 9 with a foolproof method, immune from occasional setbacks. It does mean you will have a solid framework to guide you through the decisions necessary for successful implementation of whatever computer applications you consider important.

WORLD'S SHORTEST COURSE
ON EDUCATIONAL CHANGE

Before launching into the details of planning your change effort, it's critical to have a firm grasp, as the Cheshire Cat recommends, of where you want to go. Various models of educational change all attempt to point that way. To keep things simple and straightforward, think of your path being divided into three general phases: planning, implementation, and incorporation.

Planning begins with a set of forces (such as your P.T.O.'s recent computer purchase) setting the process in motion, and culminates with a decision regarding adoption of your proposal. Assuming your district decision-makers give the green light to adopt the computer application under consideration, you find yourself faced with the prospect of implementing what you've just adopted.

Implementation refers to the actual use of the computer application in your school. This use may vary from teacher to teacher, and may differ from the formal plan. In fact, full scale implementation of the plan typically takes three to five years before a majority of the teachers are using the computer application as designed. This shouldn't be construed negatively. Simply, it's a realistic perspective on what your expectations should be regarding the change effort.

The incorporation phase of the project occurs when the computer application becomes a part of the routine patterns of the user. That is, the application is stabilized, few if any changes are being made in ongoing use, and little thought or preparation is being given to improving the computer application. At this point, in all likelihood, the curriculum is no longer considered "new." It is a standard part of the repertoire of the teacher or administrator.

With this brief primer on educational change as backdrop, let's go back to the beginning, the planning phase of your project.

HELPFUL HINTS FOR TAKING THOSE IMPORTANT FIRST STEPS

When the excitement is high and momentum is building for a fresh, new look in the form of computer technology, the temptation may be to jump into the "doing" aspects of the project before laying the proper foundation. What follows is a series of steps to ensure that your project gets started on the right foot.

Step One: Specify the priority computer applications. Returning to the process outlined in Chapter 6, make sure you have followed a systematic procedure for identifying the priority computer applications. Once you have determined the cost effective uses of computer technology, and have ordered them according to importance, you have taken a critical first step in laying the foundation for *why* you are proceeding on a particular course. When the critics start crawling from the woodwork to lobby for their pet applications or challenge the wisdom of yours, you're prepared with a rationale for why you've singled out certain computer applications as most important.

Speaking of critics, you need to weigh carefully which audiences you plan to involve in the priority-setting process. Generally, sound planning entails gathering ideas from all of the major groups affected by the change. In the case of planning for computer technology, your decision is complicated by the specialized nature of computers. To seek input from parents, students, and other interested groups is to risk having uninformed opinion dictate how computers should be used. On the other hand, these groups will be affected by the eventual decision. Perhaps the best planning strategy is to first work through the steps outlined in Chapter 6 with those staff members most responsible for implementing the proposed change and arrive at a set of recommendations you can defend and support. Next, meet with those groups you consider important in helping shape the decisions; with these groups, discuss how and why you arrived at your particular recommendations. Be prepared to alter your final recommendations, however, based on the feedback from these meetings.

Step Two: Secure the necessary resource commitments. Using the worksheet approach in Chapter 6, you can arrive at a reasonable estimate of the costs incurred to plan and implement your computer application. Therefore, you have documentation explaining estimated expenditures for equipment, maintenance, repair, software, and staff development. Before you advance the project much further, however, you need to make sure you have the money and human resources to complete what you set out to do. Many of the projects in the "innovation graveyard" died from a lack of funding. In particular, numerous computer-related projects have been terminated because school officials failed to consider what they would do when external funds ran out. For the sake of your own change effort, as well as the overall reputation of computer technology in schools, it's imperative you gain a firm commitment from those controlling the purse strings—a promise that the resources will be there during the entire course of planning and implementing your project.

Step Three: Identify your project's organizational structure. A key to success in putting computer power in the schools is to have a clearly conceptualized organizational structure before wading too deeply into the development aspects of your project. Most planning models outline three levels of organizational structure. First, at the "grass roots" level, teachers assume primary responsibility for planning and implementing a new idea, either in their own classrooms or on behalf of their school. This organizational structure has greatest appeal when the computer application is confined to a school or particular classrooms. For example, if a school decides to implement computer managed instruction (CMI), it seems most productive to establish an organizational structure governed by those directly affected by the CMI system, including principal, teachers, and possibly students or parents. In the Sherman School Project, a glaring finding from the evaluation data was that parents had little understanding of CMI's effects on their child's schooling. Building parents into the organizational structure during the planning phase might alleviate some potential communication problems later.

At the second level, educational change occurs from the top down. In extreme cases, school district officials decide certain computer applications are best, and they design a process to see that it happens. Under these circumstances, the change as designed rarely looks anything like the change as implemented. Teachers are able to adapt a proposed change effort to fit their needs, even if it means distorting the original idea drastically. More frequently, top-down change happens when a core group of administrators, teachers, and others are assembled to plan for the intended change, leaving details of implementation to the users. This organizational structure builds on some input from various interest groups, but it can cut off communication from the rank and file. It's very difficult, for instance, to expect a handful of teachers serving on a committee to adequately represent their colleagues' perspectives. Instead, the planners end up representing their personal viewpoints only.

A third level of organizational structure, the cooperative planning level, links the users of the computer application directly with designated representatives from each school involved in the project. These representatives from teacher and administrative ranks (plus parents and students, if appropriate) comprise the task force, a group ultimately responsible for decision-making. Within the task force, a core group of teachers and administrators operates as a steering committee. This nucleus group meets frequently, working through the details associated with planning, as well as initially presenting ideas for the task force to consider. The task force members, in turn, solicit feedback from their constituency and enter this information into the planning, as well as initially presenting ideas for the task force to consider. The task force members, in turn, solicit feedback from their constituency and enter this information into the planning process. As illustrated in Figure 9-1, the cooperative planning model builds in regular communication with all teachers who will use the computer applications.

FIGURE 9-1. COOPERATIVE PLANNING MODEL

**Project Users
(All teachers and administrators
in the project)**

Task Force

**Steering Committee
(Selected teachers and
administrators from the task force)**

(Teacher and administration representatives from all schools in the computer project; also curriculum consultants and specialists, as necessary)

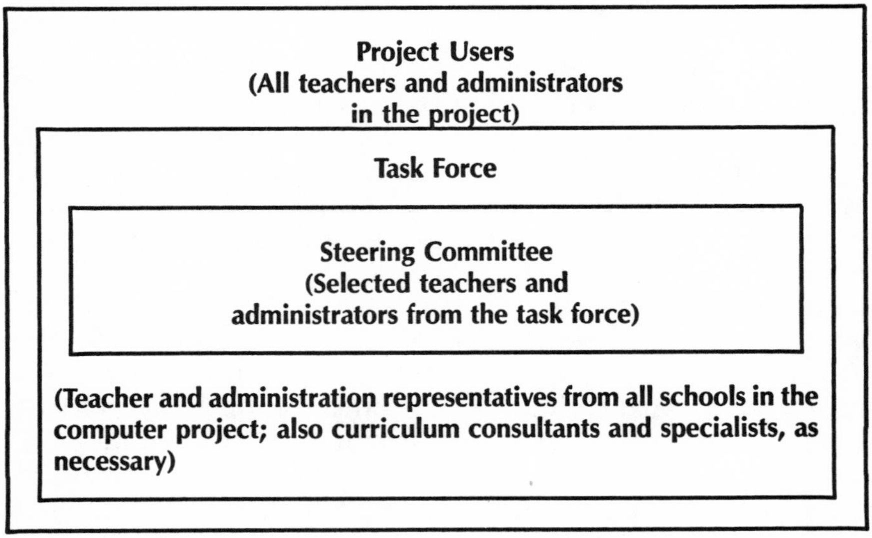

While not foolproof, this organizational structure seems to combine the best of both worlds: All teachers and administrators have access to the planning process, while final recommendations are made by the task force members who have worked most closely with the planning process. No single organizational structure best serves all computer planning needs. You need to assess which structure offers you the most powerful planning model, keeping in mind the need to somehow include those ultimately responsible for implementing the plan.

FOUR CRITICAL FACTORS
SHAPING THE QUALITY OF IMPLEMENTATION

Until recently, the emphasis during educational change efforts was heavy on the planning phase, leaving implementation to the doers. The prevailing thought seemed to be that if planning was done on a first-rate basis, first-rate implementation just naturally followed. Several research studies later, we have learned things don't usually work out this way. In fact, effective planning involves careful attention to the details of implementing the project long before any actual use of the new program takes place. In particular, four factors stand out as primary elements shaping the change effort for which you are planning. Each of these factors is outlined below.

Teacher Motivation for Implementing a Project

By pinpointing the motivation for implementing a project, you can predict the likelihood of eventual success of the change effort. Drawing from a massive study of Federal projects, investigators found that projects started for political or opportunistic reasons were rarely implemented effectively. In other words, if you're motivated to implement CAL because influential community leaders pressed for it, or because you had to spend $10,000 in Federal funds or lose the money, you're unlikely to have the necessary commitment required for successful implementation. In instances such as these, the implementers of the curriculum, usually teachers, have no ownership in the product or process of arriving at implementation. They go along with the project to avoid penalties, the withholding of organizational rewards for not complying with implementation as intended.

Another motivation for implementing a project grows out of the derived benefits. There may be virtually no commitment to the project per se, but implementation of a computer application may bring with it other rewards such as new teaching materials. As an example, you may find that teachers aren't really that interested in the instructional features of computer technology; they are interested, however, in the payoff of having some help in their teaching activities. Even though the derived benefit can be a sufficient motivation to bring about implementation, the quality of the computer application remains open to question. A desire to improve the quality of the school program serves as a third motivation during the implementation phase. In cases where needs have been clearly identified and teachers want to take steps to improve their program, such motivations can be a powerful incentive for teachers spending their scarce energy in implementing something as new and different as computer technology.

A common mistake made in preparing for implementation is to ignore teacher needs as a motivation, and instead assume they will implement the curriculum because somebody else decides it's necessary. In reality, this isn't the case. To summarize, you need to carefully examine the motivation factor that's built into the planning process—if you want to maximize the payoff that comes when teachers implement something they're excited about.

Taking Stock of How Teachers Participate in Implementation

If a program is implemented in some fashion, almost by definition the teachers participate in using it. The issue centers on how they use it. Some planners view implementation as synonymous with installation; a switch is flipped to the "on" position, then teachers are expected to begin implementing. They assume a rather passive role in the process. Alternatively, teacher participation can take the form of involvement or input into decisions affecting implementation. One major review of research on this subject (McLaughlin and Marsh, 1978), found that teachers didn't have opportunities for participation on a regular basis during implementation. The researchers found that teachers, because of their day-to-day involvement with project operations, are in a better position than district specialists or even the project director to identify problems and recommend feasible solutions. Realistically, teachers are going to customize the computer application anyway. They might as well transform their expertise and experience into shaping the official curriculum, as opposed to just shaping the curriculum in use.

The Effects of School Setting on Implementation

Participation in the implementation of a project occurs within a school setting that is peculiar to the time, place, and people involved in the process. A major influential factor is what has been labeled "school culture." The norms, incentives, and history of the school all combine to have an effect on the success rate of implementation. For instance, a school's history of successful implementation efforts has a direct bearing on the probability of success for the computer application you have in mind. Another element of history worth noting is the process normally used to achieve implementation. If, for example, your school is accustomed to a school-based approach to implementing programs, there's a good chance your school culture would be adversely affected by an imposition of a top-down implementation plan, even if such a plan had been effective in other parts of the district. The norms and values of a school are also powerful forces shaping implementation. Specifically, the culture of the school imposes certain constraints on individual teacher behavior. Teachers have some latitude behind the classroom door, until what they do runs counter to the established ways of the school. At this point, the norms and values tend to pull and tug the individual toward a position of conformity. By being sensitive to the setting where your computer project will take place, you can improve the odds of successful implementation.

The Role of Leadership in the Implementation Process

During implementation, leadership shifts from the initiators, planners, and developers to the school principal (Czajkowski and Patterson, 1980). The facilitators of projects are only minimally effective in implementation, while the principal becomes a major influence.

Principals have a significant impact on program improvement through their influence on school climate and their posture regarding the computer project being implemented. In particular, the principal is chiefly responsible for setting the tone and policy of the school. To the extent that the tone of a school reflects good working relationships among teachers and a willingness to struggle openly and honestly with issues, the school is more likely to achieve successful implementation. Principals also send important messages to teachers with their behavior and involvement in the project. One study found, for instance, that when teachers detected the principal disliked the project, project outcomes were almost always unfavorable. In other words, the more supportive the principal is perceived to be, the greater the chances for successful implementation of the project. In summary, the principal can give moral support to the staff and create a school climate that gives the project legitimacy.

The leadership skills of the principal also play a prominent role in implementation. A protracted discussion of the leadership skills necessary to make the computer application come alive in the school—for example, active involvement by the principal, a thorough knowledge of the computer application by the principal, and systematic monitoring of the new project—extends beyond the scope of this section; nevertheless, they at least deserve to be mentioned because of the critical role they play in the implementation phase.

None of the factors outlined above provide you with a cookbook approach to effective implementation of your project. It would be naive to pretend that there is one best recipe. But it isn't naive, indeed it's very wise, to understand how the interplay of factors just

FIGURE 9-2. STAGES OF CONCERN (SoC) FRAMEWORK*

<u>STAGE</u>	<u>DESCRIPTION</u>
0. Awareness	Little concern about the innovation is indicated. The person doesn't feel that it has any implications for him or her.
1. Informational	A general awareness of the innovation and interest in learning more about it are expressed.
2. Personal	Uncertainty is acknowledged about the demands of the innovation, along with inadequacy to meet those demands. Concerns at this stage usually reflect self-doubts and lack of confidence with respect to the innovation.
3. Management	Attention is focused on the processes and tasks of using the innovation. Concerns are expressed about the logistics and time required by the person in relation to the innovation.
4. Consequence	Concerns are indicated about how the innovation is affecting the learner. The focus is on the relevance of the innovation for students, the evaluation of student outcomes, and the changes needed to increase student outcomes.
5. Collaboration	The focus is on coordination and cooperation with others regarding the use of the innovation. The individual is interested in improving student learning by pooling talents and resources.

6. Refocusing	The attention turns to an exploration of major changes, with the possibility of replacing the innovation with a more powerful alternative. He or she has definite ideas about alternatives to the proposed or existing form of the innovation.

Source: Hall, G., A. George, and W. Rutherford, *Measuring Stages of Concern About the Innovation: A Manual for Use of the SoC Questionnaire,* Austin: The Research and Development Center for Teacher Education, University of Texas at Austin, 1977.

described comes to bear on the ultimate success or failure of implementing the various computer applications you have selected.

RESOLVING TEACHER AND ADMINISTRATOR CONCERNS ABOUT USING COMPUTERS

As you move from planning to implementation, you will face the inevitable challenge of allaying concerns about this new innovation called computers. Whether we are just being introduced to the idea of computers or we immerse ourselves in this technology on a regular basis, we experience a series of concerns calling for resolution. The purpose of this section is to provide you with a framework for understanding and resolving concerns about using computers in schools.

The framework we use identifies seven different stages of concern a person goes through when dealing with an innovation. In the case of the innovation of using computers in schools, teachers move through the stages described in Figure 9-2 in a roughly linear pattern. Using the stages of concern (SoC) framework to illustrate the point, teachers usually have awareness, informational, and personal concerns. Until these concerns are reckoned with, "higher order" concerns (e.g., management, consequence) are not an issue. But it is important to recognize that there is no value attached to having some concerns over others.

Developmentally, we all wrestle with informational and personal concerns before we experience management concerns as the most dominant state. Also, in most instances, we simultaneously have several concerns operating at the same time. It is just that some are more intense than others.

To illustrate how the stages of concern framework can be applied to a school setting, let's take a hypothetical case of Mr. George Severs, a fifth-grade teacher at Barber Elementary. Suppose the school principal received notice that the local Parent Teacher Organization is willing to spend $500 on a microcomputer. Most likely, Mr. Severs will begin with some awareness concerns and move rather quickly to informational concerns. Typical expressions of concern at this stage are: "I would like to know more about microcomputers. I don't really understand how the machines work. One thing's for sure, though, I can't make intelligent decisions about using the micro without a better understanding than I have now."

Soon the micro arrives at school, and the principal announces that all students should have some hands-on experience with the computer before the end of the school year. Now Mr. Severs begins to feel the intensity of personal concerns. Examples of this stage are contained in statements like: "I'm not clear how this machine is going to affect me. What will I have to give up in the summer in order to spend time with this? I'm also concerned about the possibility of technology replacing teacher."

Two weeks later, the principal asks Mr. Severs to try having students load and save programs, keeping track of student reactions so the principal and Mr. Severs can discuss these points. Even though informational and personal concerns have not disappeared, management concerns appear as most intense now. This is evident in comments like: "I'm not sure how I can work this into my already cramped schedule. Even if I can, managing this learning center with all the other things going on will be tough. There just aren't enough hours in the day to get these centers running smoothly."

Without taking the scenario through each subsequent stage, in all likelihood Mr. Severs eventually will feel more in control of this innovation and management concerns will subside. Then he will begin to turn his attention toward making the technology pay off in terms of improved student learning, reflected in Figure 9-2 as consequence concerns. When consequence concerns are more intense than other stages, typical expressions of concerns are: "How is my use affecting kids? What are the most important computer literacy goals? I'm wondering how I can change things so more students can get access to the micros."

The stages of concern (SoC) framework offers the teacher and administrator a way to conceptualize people's feelings as they move through the adoption and implementation of an innovation. More importantly, the research in this area points to the need for teachers and administrators to understand that it is acceptable to have a range of concerns about using computers, and that it is natural for people being introduced to computer technology to find personal concerns very intense at the outset. The key to successful implementation is determining which concerns about an innovation are most pressing at the moment, then offering ways to help resolve these concerns.

One of the most direct ways to measure teacher concerns about computer technology is to listen, ask questions, and observe teacher comments. This strategy can give you valuable insights about what may be on a given teacher's mind. Another way is to administer a more formal survey, gathering written feedback from teachers. Once you have collected the information, the next obvious but not so easy task is to work closely with staff members to reduce their present concerns. In the language of one researcher (Hall, 1979), "interventions" are made to help resolve their concerns. These interventions take different forms, depending on the concern identified. For persons with high informational concerns, interventions must be targeted to provide very general descriptive information. The following types of interventions might be effective:

- Circulate descriptions of orientation sessions for teachers regarding computers.
- Provide an opportunity to visit other classrooms where computers are being used.
- Conduct a question-and-answer period with teachers in a safe environment where they understand that no question is considered too silly.

In contrast, persons with relatively intense management concerns need supportive interventions such as:

- Provide help in ways that address the specific "how-to" issues causing the concern.
- Have other teachers share their successful and unsuccessful practices.
- Create a support group so teachers can share with each other their concerns about logistics, time, etc.

Even though these examples barely scratch the surface, they serve to illustrate that the intensity and nature of concerns about computers vary with time and across individuals; it is all right for teachers to be concerned about the effect of this innovation on their own lives before they can turn attention to the world of students; and finally, resolving teacher concerns requires an understanding of the stages of concern, as well as the realization that successful interventions require a range of strategies, depending on which teacher concerns are most intense at the moment. One set of strategies, designing a comprehensive staff development program, is described in the next section.

BUILDING STAFF DEVELOPMENT INTO YOUR PLANNING EFFORTS

Back in the old days, staff development equaled training. Teachers and administrators spent precious preservice and in-service time learning the trade. Now things are different. No longer are we faced with training new teachers on a large scale. Instead our ranks are filled with veterans who likely have been in the same school for several years. They have had more than their share of sitting through sessions designed to fix their teaching, their students, or their overall view of how children learn. Keeping this in mind, it's possible to design a staff development program that responds sensitively to the needs teachers and administrators themselves identify as important.

The specific makeup of your staff development efforts will vary with the type of computer application implemented. For example, the scope of staff development needed to achieve teacher computer literacy in a school district is far different from the staff development required to help a school implement computer managed instruction. To help you in the planning process, this section poses staff development issues you need to consider for each of the major computer applications described in this book.

At the least, computer assisted learning requires the teacher to be knowledgeable about how to operate computer equipment. Otherwise, it proves inefficient, ineffective, and plain inexcusable when the teacher can't operate the computer he or she expects the student to use. Another need of teachers implementing CAL is a thorough knowledge of available software, especially how to evaluate for effectiveness the flood of computer programs on the market. Until the teacher demonstrates mastery of running the computer and selecting quality software, the effective implementation of CAL remains problematic.

Staff development requirements inherent in using computer managed instruction are less rigorous. Most examples of CMI in action underscore the need for someone to be specially trained in how to get student information into and out of the computer. Often, a school aide serves in this role. Good planning also dictates that at least one other person, serving as a backup, knows how to perform these functions. Classroom teachers, on the other hand, need to know how to interpret the data such as those illustrated in Chapter 4. Beyond the ability to effectively use output from the computer to manage instructional activities, classroom teachers need very little working knowledge of the intricacies involved in computer technology.

When implementing computer technology for administrative purposes, only a handful of people need intensive staff development. In this case, training may be a more apt description of what takes place. As an illustration, suppose you want to use the computer for word processing in the office. Staff development would entail having the principal and secretary, for instance, spending a block of time, perhaps two full days, learning to master the system. This type of learning wouldn't resemble very much the type of learning that would occur in a computer literacy workshop for teachers. In other words, staff development for administrative uses is more specialized. It requires the user to engage intensely in how to use the computer as a tool to perform the specific administrative function required.

Tackling computer literacy demands varying staff development approaches, depending on the selected definition of literacy. To illustrate the point, let's look at different scenarios of how computer literacy is handled.

First, assume your district has declared that computer literacy should be taught in Grades 7 through 12, with a heavy emphasis placed at two checkpoints, a computer awareness course in Grade 8 and a computer programming course in Grade 11. The balance of the objectives should be integrated into the regular curriculum. Now the problem comes in trying to decide which teachers should participate in computer literacy staff development activities and how much exposure they need. At the least, teachers must be thoroughly schooled in the computer literacy objectives targeted for their respective grade levels. For instance, if a primary student objective at Grade 9 is to learn various career opportunities requiring skills in computer technology, then the classroom teacher has a challenging staff development assignment. He or she needs to stay current on the rapidly changing field of computer-related careers. To do this, an ongoing staff development program needs to be made available for these teachers. More desirable than just having teachers prepared to address the limited number of objectives at the various grade levels is the goal of having all staff members as computer literate as the graduating students. Such a position calls for a more comprehensive, broad-based staff development program. It means engaging all teachers sytematically in a long-range program. If you choose to move in this direction, a quick review of current educational computer journals will yield numerous models for staff development that have worked well for other school districts.

A different dilemma emerges when your district isn't currently treating computer literacy as a priority for students, but teachers feel themselves quickly losing ground in the computer literacy race. No doubt, you've witnessed individual pleas made by teachers who clamor for all of the literacy training they can devour. Other teachers keep their fingers crossed that "This too shall pass." Do you require, that is, force, all teachers to participate in a staff development program? Do you offer something only for those who are ready to move forward? Or do you mandate awareness level activities, leaving subsequent sessions to those who volunteer? As you contemplate their choices leading to final action, keep these points in mind:

- Staff development in education is not synonymous with personnel training in business. Unlike business, in education it's rare that we can define specific skills which, if mastered, will guarantee more productivity, for example, improved student learning.
- Teachers and administrators, like students, learn better when they see a need or purpose for learning.
- Time is a precious commodity for educators. If you engage in a plan to spend this precious commodity of teachers and administrators, make sure it is well spent. It's being used on staff development at the expense of something else in the classroom or school being shortchanged.
- If you mandate a staff development program, involve teachers and administrators heavily in the planning. Also keep the communication lines open with the audience of the staff development program. Even if they don't agree with your plan, they should at least understand why it's being implemented and what it's intended to accomplish.

In summary, to be effective, teachers need to have a strong sense of efficacy, a feeling of control over the forces affecting the learning in the classroom. Staff development can be the vital tool teachers can call on as they see a need to renew, refresh, and regenerate. As a planner, your attention to effective staff development strategies can make a world of difference in the success of your computer application.

SUCCESSFULLY MANAGING THE IMPLEMENTATION OF COMPUTER TECHNOLOGY

Too often, stories have been told of the energetic P.T.O. rushing to buy a computer or two for the school, while unprepared principals and staff members scratch their collective heads wondering, "What do we do once the thing arrives?" Without putting undue restraint on the parents excited about computers in the school, you need to stall long enough so that you can work through many of the management issues swirling around the introduction of new computer equipment into your school. To help you with this management planning, the following questions are presented for your deliberation. Other questions inevitably will arise, but your prepared response to these issues will at least get you started in the right direction.

What Is the Primary Use of the Computer Equipment?

Hopefully, this question has been answered long before you get to this point. But the answer regarding purpose shapes the answers to all of the subsequent questions. When you've clearly described primary use, you're ready to move to the next set of questions.

Where Will the Computer Be Used?

Obviously, the answer depends on how you want to use it. Except for the designated use of administrative applications, the computer needs to be located close to students and teachers. Options to consider include the library, a computer center, a movable center on carts, and a supervised checkout room. Assuming you don't have enough computers to permanently station them in each classroom or cluster of classrooms, you face the task of maximizing the use of this scarce and demanded resource. Your final answer hinges on other management issues.

Where Can the Power Supply Requirements Be Met?

Suppose you decide that, ideally, your four computers should be in the library. Before moving too hastily, you should determine if you have adequate power outlets and if the electrical power source is reliable. Imagine how discouraging it would be to have the library rearranged to make room for the computers, only to find out that the electrical circuits can't handle the power requirements.

Who's in Charge?

This means two things: who is responsible for supervising the computer application in your school, and who is personally accountable for the computer equipment? If the same person is in charge of both, it's likely that he or she would want the equipment close to his or her professional home base. For example, if the librarian assumes responsibility for the equipment, that reason may be compelling enough to place the equipment in the library. Whatever your final answer, it is highly recommended that someone have clear authority to take charge of the project. Otherwise the project can drift aimlessly into nonexistence. Given the financial investment you've made, it's also imperative that a designated person account for the presence and condition of the equipment. Answers to these questions need to be agreed on in the planning process, long before the computers arrive ready to go to work.

What Is the Scheduling Process?

If the computer needs to be shared by several users, some plan must be devised for getting the most mileage out of the equipment. One elementary principal distributed a form, shown in Figure 9-3, to all staff members at the beginning of the school year. The principal could use the completed forms to build a schedule for the best use of time. However handled, the schedule will ultimately be shaped by factors such as the number of hours the computer is available daily, staff members or other adults who can supervise activities, and which students have access to the computer. In some high schools, only students carrying special passes can schedule time at the computer center.

What Security Measures Have Been Taken?

Provision for the protection of both equipment and software should be a priority item in the planning process. Most schools find a room away from the flow of traffic to lock equipment and software each night. Only designated personnel have keys to this room. Also, some districts use check-out systems so teachers and stu-

FIGURE 9-3. MICROCOMPUTER REQUEST FORM

---

1. I would like to request the micro for:

       _____2 days

       _____1 week

       _____3 weeks

       _____Other

2. I would like to take the micro home to "tinker around."

       _____Yes

       _____No

3. I would like to try the following activities with my class:

4. I need the following resources or help in preparation for using the micro:

       TEACHER   **DATE**

---

dents can borrow equipment overnight, on weekends, and during vacations. This system provides greater opportunities for learning, and reduces the security problems inherent in having expensive equipment in an empty building. Having an equipment and software checklist attached to a cart is critical if the computer is moved frequently during the day. It's also a good idea to permanently mark all equipment for easy identification. Another form of security deserves mention at this point. If you are using a time-sharing system for your computer needs, careful attention should be given to the security of data on the mainframe computer. Typically, this is handled via password codes, allowing only authorized users to enter the data base. Given the strict confidentiality rules in most school districts, data security is not a topic to be passed over lightly.

What Are the Provisions for Repair and Maintenance?

Many school districts are moving quickly to train their own technicians to service computer equipment. This makes a lot of sense financially, especially if you have several computers in your district. Your decision on this issue will also be affected by the availability of service locally. If you are in close proximity to a service center, it may be more economical to take the computer in for repair. Another consideration is how long you will be without a computer. If the computer service center is willing to loan you equipment until yours is repaired, this will save you precious computer time. Finally, you may find it more advantageous to sign a service contract with a vendor than to pay for training your own technicians. Whatever your ultimate decison, it should be made before the computer arrives and maintenance or repair becomes urgent.

As you formulate answers to these and related questions regarding the management of the computer application you implement, your uppermost goal should be the reasonable "care and feeding" of the equipment, without unduly restricting its use by students and adults. By letting these questions guide you in your planning, you can expect many productive years from your new computer technology.

But how many years ahead should you be planning? Can your current plan of action carry you forward, or do you need to modify your plan commensurate with the rapid changes in the field of computer technology? Chapter 10 gives you a glimpse of the future to help you form your own vision of things to come.

CHAPTER 9 REFERENCES

Carroll, Lewis, *The Annotated Alice: Alice's Adventures in Wonderland and Through the Looking Glass*, New York: Clarkson Potter Publishing, 1960.

Czajkowski, Theodore J., and Jerry L. Patterson, "Curriculum Change and the Schools," in *Considered Action for Curriculum Improvement*, A. W. Foshay (ed.), Alexandria, Va.: Association for Supervision and Curriculum Development Yearbook, 1980.

Dickerson, L., and W. H. Pritchard, "Microcomputers and Education: Planning for the Coming Revolution in the Classroom," *Educational Technology*, Jan. 1981.

Diem, R. A., "Developing Computer Education Skills: An Inservice Training Program," *Educational Technology*, Feb. 1981.

Hall, G. E., "Issues Related to the Implementation of Computers in Classrooms," *The Journal of Computers in Mathematics and Science Teaching*, 1981.

Hall, G. E., A. A. George, and W. L. Rutherford, *Measuring Stages of Concern About the Innovation: A Manual for Use of the SoC Questionnaire*, Austin, TX: Research and Development Center for Teacher Education, The University of Texas, 1977.

Hall, G. E., and W. L. Rutherford, "Concerns of Teachers About Implementing Team Teaching," *Educational Leadership*, Dec. 1976.

Kepner, H., Jr., *Computers in the Classroom*, Washington, DC: National Education Association, 1982.

McLaughlin, M. W., and D. D. Marsh, "Staff Development and School Change," *Teachers College Record*, Sept. 1978, p. 69.

1983 Classroom Computer News Directory of Educational Computing Resources, Watertown, MA: Intentional Educations, Inc., 1983.

Olds, H. F., Jr., "Teaching the Teachers: An Inservice Syllabus," *Classroom Computer News*, Sept./Oct. 1981.

Pratscher, S., "Planning for Microcomputers in the Classroom," *The Journal of Computers in Mathematics and Science Teaching*, Fall 1981.

10

ANTICIPATING THE FUTURE

Let your imagination have free rein for a moment. Suppose a world summit meeting of nationally acclaimed experts just adjourned. At a press conference called to discuss the meeting, the presiding officer of the conference revealed a revolutionary breakthrough in education. Following is a transcript of his hypothetical statement.

> Over the past several weeks, we have been charged with the enormous task of sifting through relevant research to pinpoint any connection between the newly discovered Marcuvian language, brain research, and learning. I have the honor of unveiling our results.

> First, we have unquestionably concluded that the Marcuvian language is the single most powerful vehicle our civilization possesses for teaching all citizens, particularly our children, to think in logical, problem-solving modes. Simply by mastering this language, students have the capabilities to conceptualize, problem solve, and communicate in ways unheard of until now. We're convinced that the Marcuvian language can be mastered by virtually all students before they graduate from high school.

Second, our analysis of brain periodization, hemispheric, and related research reveals a definite link between thinking skills and Marcuvian language acquisition. Students who master the Marcuvian language have a far superior repertoire of skills and learning to take with them into the world of work and advanced study. Furthermore, it's our firm conviction that this language will become the dominant mode of communication by the most advanced sectors of our society. To get ahead, both professionally and socially, students will need a command of this language.

Finally, I'm pleased to announce that our conference proceedings included time to develop a device that will not only teach you how to learn the language; it will allow you to communicate via Marcuvian language with others throughout the country having a similar device. All you need to do is learn how to operate the equipment, once you have learned the language. With sufficient training, students will greet entire new vistas in thinking and learning. The world of the future belongs to those who master the Marcuvian language.

Suppose the spokesperson is right in his claims. Continuing to let your imagination rule, consider the applications such a pronouncement bodes for education. To capitalize on the power packed into the newly discovered Marcuvian language and its hold on success for individuals, we have no choice in education. In the long-range best interest of students, educators need to take whatever steps necessary to see that students leave school with a mastery of the Marcuvian language. Such steps include rethinking what's important for students to learn, retraining teachers to teach accordingly, and reordering priorities that direct the distribution of monetary and human resources.

Moving now from a fantasy world to the real world of education, suddenly we're faced with a Marcuvian language of our own. We're experiencing a force that possesses the power to reshape our children's present education and future world. Whereas we can read a fictitious account of the Marcuvian language and respond in a calculated, analytical fashion, our response to the real world of computers is different. We have some hint of its powerful capabilities. We have an even stronger sense of our inadequacies. We have emotion about this technology that interferes with our rational processes that tell us how best to proceed. But we have to proceed. To help get started, Chapter 10 looks into the future of computer technology. Acknowledging the inevitable imprecision of forecasting and speculating, this chapter draws on what we know up to this point, to give you sound guidance about what to expect in the future. An attempt is made to restrain emotion, giving rationality a little more running room.

SHORT-TERM PLANS VS. LONG-RANGE PLANNING

The purpose of this book, at least 90 percent of it, is to give you a framework for putting computer power in the schools. This framework stands on the assumption that you need to act rather soon. Unlike the Marcuvian language, computer technology really exists and it possesses a power being demonstrated in school districts throughout the country. The step-by-step approach in this book will help you move effectively from virtually no understanding of computer technology to a point where you successfully implement the computer applications you feel are most important in your setting. Whether you reach this point in six months or three years, you have really just begun the planning process. You have engaged in short-term plans, using today's technology and today's demands, to put computer power in your school. But short-term plans are acceptable, even vital when introducing a real Marcuvian language to education. You have to start someplace. Once underway, you need to shift gears toward a long-range plan. Today's technology and needs won't stand the test of time. Your challenge is similar to the one presented in the vignette: In the long-range best interest of students, we need to take whatever steps are necessary to see that students leave school with an understanding of computer technology. Such steps include rethinking what's important for students to learn, retraining teachers to teach accordingly, and reordering priorities that direct the distribution of resources. The balance of this chapter incorporates these steps into a projection of future trends in computer technology.

KEEPING UP WITH CHANGES IN HARDWARE

If you feel you're losing ground when it comes to understanding computer hardware, you aren't alone. Computer science specialists who devote their careers to this field acknowledge that the pace is too rapid for them to stay current in their specialty. In a school district, you certainly can justify at least one person designated as computer coordinator who would assume responsibility for staying on top of events and discoveries in the field. Technical advice, then, could be directed to the person in the computer coordinator role. But this person alone can't carry the load. You need a district perspective on what to expect from the hardware of the future. This section helps sharpen your perspective.

To begin with, predictions about downward spiraling prices on computer equipment have held true—to a point. In the last few years, you've witnesseed a dramatic drop in computer prices. The rate of decrease is slowing, however. That is, even though the absolute price of a computer continues to decline, the decrease isn't as marked as it was a short time ago. A major reason is the stable, if not increasing, price of labor and manufacturing materials. The unit price of metal, plastic, and related materials likely won't turn downward, even with improved computer technology. So what you can expect, in the next several years, is a leveling off of the price for a designated computer unit.

Even with relatively stable prices for the microcomputer you are contemplating, you can expect to get more for your money. As technology continues to improve, you can buy more power for the same price. Expanded memory, as well as more preprogrammed chips, gives you much more power packed into the same computer housing. For example, for $500, you can get a machine in the future that will resemble your current computer in appearance and price, but tomorrow's computer will drastically outperform today's model. A major contributor to your improved computing power can be traced to more powerful microprocessor chips. Advanced technology will allow you to put more preprogrammed instructions into your computer, thereby giving you more memory space for your own programming. Also, these chips can be programmed to do a lot of the "thinking" you had formerly been required to do.

Two other hardware changes are on the horizon. First of all, you will see a breakthrough in the display capabilities of computers. For most of the microcomputers currently on the market, the typical display screen takes the form of a TV-type monitor. In some cases, the cost of the monitor exceeds the cost of the computer itself. Many schools have gotten excited because they could finally purchase a $200 microcomputer, only to discover that the cost of the accessories more than doubled the price of the computer. With refinements in the liquid crystal display (LCD), the cost of the display device will drop the price of the computer package to a much more affordable price-range for schools. This translates into more computers for more schools.

Alternatives to the one computer/one disk drive unit can also dramatically affect prices. For most computer applications, access to a disk drive becomes an eventual necessity. Like conventional display screens, however, the price of disk drives exceeds the cost of many computers, and puts the total package price of computer systems out of the reach of many school budgets. With advances in technology, the pricing structure for output devices can also be improved. As an illustration, consider the effect that networking has had on costs. In instances where schools have hooked up a dozen or more computers to a master disk drive, the cost of external storage per station dropped significantly.

As you can tell from the brief outline just given, hardware costs for microcomputers will continue their downward trend, putting microcomputer power within the reach of more schools than ever.

Another form of computer power is now available to schools. For less than $100 per unit, schools can purchase hand-held computers having many of the capabilities of their larger relatives. However, the hand-held computer sacrifices memory and display space to achieve its goal of computer power in small packages. But even the hand-held models can be upgraded via hookup to larger display devices and mass storage devices.

Another technology that holds promise for classroom use is the videodisc, a plastic storage and retrieval medium about the size of an LP record. Each side of the disc contains 54,000 separate frames in the form of images, pictures, or other information. This information is read by a laser beam, so unlike a record player's needle, no physical contact is made between laser beam and videodisc—allowing you to use the disc indefinitely, without concern over wearing it out. Another feature of this technology is the ability to find any piece of information on the disc in a matter of seconds. Thus you can store and retrieve moving pictures, still pictures, words, or other symbols with amazing speed. You can also hold motionless any one of the 54,000 frames.

But what does such a media marvel have to do with computers and education? Plenty. Currently, computer educators are exploring the instructional implications of linking the videodisc and microcomputer. With this configuration, the user can interact with computer technology in new and exciting ways. Suppose, for instance, a student wants to participate in a simulation showing how to dissect a crayfish in science class. Combining computer and videodisc technology, the student receives instruction via the videodisc, complete with actual visual images of the crayfish in various phases of dissection. Using the power of the computer, the student controls the lesson, stopping at any frame for as long as necessary, or backing up to a point previously made.

Another advantage of the videodisc is its ability to combine the mediums of words and images into one package. Assuming that each frame of a videodisc holds ten words, the two sides of a disc house more than 1 million words, equivalent to a volume of books containing over 2,500 pages. In other words, you can provide your student a complete set of encyclopedias by supplying him with one videodisc.

As you might guess, cost is one of the major drawbacks to putting videodisc technology in schools. At the present time, the costs to design, produce, and prepare a master disc exceed $50,000. A computer-controlled videodisc player runs about $2,000, with individual discs costing about $25. When school district officials add all of the figures, they must include the cost of the microcomputer equipment as well as the cost of the videodisc technology. Once again, district decision-makers face the inevitable question: Is this technology cost effective? By making a cost comparison between the per word or image cost of other media with videodiscs linked to computers, you may indeed find that you can justify a spot for this technology in your school's future.

In the near future, you will find teaching with microcomputers better adapted to students with handicaps. Imagine, for example, a student having no mobility except to wrinkle the brow being able to manipulate a computer in an instructional setting. As futuristic as this may sound, it's a reality now. By fitting the student with a special device that senses movement, the student controls the cursor on the screen and sends commands to the input device. In other classrooms, deaf students read a specially equipped computer monitor as they "listen" over loudspeakers to lectures synchronized with the printed word. Advances in computer technology have opened new vistas to these and other students who have handicaps.

In an era of scarce resources, costs become a dominant factor in deciding whether to bring computer technology to handicapped students. Clearly, the price of specially adapted computer equipment climbs higher than even conventional computers. As districts face squarely a limited budget, they must come to grips with how these scarce resources will be distributed. Will the district spend $10,000 on two pieces of equipment to help three deaf students learn more effectively—sacrificing the opportunity to buy 20 microcomputers for a computer lab in the high school? While these kinds of decisions seem harsh, they are precisely the type of issues you should be prepared for as you engage in long-range planning.

SOFTWARE OF THE FUTURE

Both the nature and quality of future software remain open to question. As discussed in Chapter 8, little incentive currently exists for publishers to plunge major investments into software development. The schools will have to greatly increase their equipment purchases before the software market will hold financial promise for commercial vendors.

Another alternative is for initiative to spring from the Federal level. If we declare computer technology a national priority (and the evidence is mounting that we should), then schools and school districts will need national support to implement the priority. This support could come in several forms, including large-scale software development projects. If, as a country, we decided to channel ample resources and our nation's talents into producing quality software to improve learning, we could move computer technology to the center stage of the classroom. Very few computer educators question the power of the computer as tutor, tool, and tutee. With increased national support to improve the quantity and quality of software, we could see a dramatic improvement in the effectiveness of computers in the schools. Just as in the Marcuvian language example, such a move requires a reordering of national priorities, along with a redistribution of monetary and human resources.

In the absence of a major push at the Federal level, the sources of software will continue to be the electronic cottage industry and in-house developments by school districts. If this holds true, you will probably see expanded offerings in the areas presently being promoted—computer assisted learning and computer literacy. This prediction could be altered, based on what you declare as tomorrow's goals.

TOMORROW'S GOALS FOR COMPUTER TECHNOLOGY

Once your short-term plans have been laid and computers are in place, it's time to begin long-range planning, leaving behind the constraints of today's technology and software. Such planning isn't easy to do. In fact, any planning that includes as many unknowns as computer technology leaves planners open to criticism from all camps, and sets up the likelihood of large margins of error because of the unknowns. But the risk of error pales compared to the potential gains from rationally and sensitively planning the course for today's students and tomorrow's leaders. Some of the futuristic questions you need to address are outlined below.

What's Important for Today's Kindergarten Students to Learn Before They Graduate from High School?

No one knows with precision the answer to this question. In fact, any answer will need to be modified with time. Regardless, this question needs to be addressed now. At the most basic level, students will need skill in operating computers, including the ability to get information into the computer, manipulate the information as necessary, and get the information out of the computer in a desirable format. While this process sounds straightforward, it requires conceptual understanding of how computers work. Storing, manipulating, and retrieving information can also be performed at various levels of sophistication. Phrased in educational jargon, computer skills are developmental and should be organized with the learner's development in mind.

Another skill demanding attention is programming. Most educators agree that some degree of programming is essential, with debate swirling around the issue of how much and in what language. As increasingly sophisticated authoring programs appear on the market, tomorrow's computer users will need less programming skill to write programs. Built into the program will be leading questions that help the user write tests, construct lessons, and individualize assignments without a command of a programming language.

The issue of which programming language to teach is also a topic for intense debate. Historically, BASIC has dominated computer applications used in education. One reason for its popularity has been its simplicity at the beginner level. Compared to other programming languages, BASIC makes the learning of simple logic possible. By writing small programs, students can learn elementary commands and see how the computer "thinks." Another mark in BASIC's favor is its roots in educational programs. Because it's the dominant language appearing in software for schools, it's the logical language for people wanting to adapt existing software to fit their needs. Continuing the cycle, because BASIC is the language educators have traditionally learned, it's the obvious choice among those expected to teach a computer language. Finally, BASIC remains popular because it can be run on computers with limited capabilities. Simple BASIC programs can be handled by computers with as little as 1K or 2K of memory, whereas other programming languages require as much as 64K of memory to run.

Despite its advantages, BASIC does have its drawbacks. As BASIC programs get more lengthy and complex, they become extremely difficult to follow—especially if you need to understand a program written by someone else. Also, BASIC isn't designed with kids in mind. To make the cursor draw a specified design, you need sophisticated programming skills. By contrast, some of the more powerful languages, like LOGO and Smalltalk, allow the student to accomplish the same results by entering one or two simple commands. Once the computer receives the command, the internal logic built into the program takes over to produce the desired result. This simplicity of use for the student is achieved at the expense of considerably more memory space needed by the language inside the computer.

For the next several years, the firm grip BASIC holds on the educational market won't be relinquished, even in the face of legitimate criticism about its power as a programming language.

Once you've decided on the language or languages in which your students should have skills, the follow-up question centers on when they should develop these skills. Although testimonials abound of young children, even preschoolers, learning to program, you should view this evidence with some caution. First of all, determine which language these youngsters used in their programming. Is this the language you've decided to teach, and can your equipment accommodate the memory requirements of the language? Secondly, find out exactly what skills are being taught. Many times it's possible to teach students by rote without their actually comprehending the concepts involved in the program they've memorized.

As students reach the middle or junior high level, developmentally most of them can handle the abstract thinking involved in simple programming. Some educators challenge this assumption, however. They claim that even a majority of high school freshmen aren't ready to think in abstract terms, operating instead at a very concrete level of thinking. In the final analysis, you should be the judge regarding the readiness of your students for the computer skills you've identified as important.

Two other factors loom important as you assess the appropriate place for teaching computer skills in tomorrow's curriculum. First, you need to consider the keyboard skills demanded by your curriculum, along with the developmental ability needed by your students to master these skills. For example, many school districts report frustration of elementary students when they have to do a lot of typing in their computer lessons. A second factor is the critical variable of interest and readiness by sex. One researcher estimates that if you divided students into those who show particular interest in learning how to program and those who do not, boys would constitute about half of the interested group in first grade, two-thirds of the interested students in sixth grade, and four-fifths of the group by the time the students reach ninth grade (Becker, 1982). Even if these figures are not precisely accurate, they call attention to the need for introducing programming skills in the curriculum before it becomes associated with an "all-boy" activity.

As you entertain the question originally posed, along with the issues just highlighted, your responses should shed some light on what computing skills today's children will need when they graduate, and where in their schooling they should acquire these skills.

Even though computer programming occupies the spotlight in any long-range planning of a computer curriculum, this topic should not be the exclusive goal of your curriculum. For instance, students should also understand how computer technology works. Thinking ahead, this means designing a curriculum with the flexibility to incorporate state-of-the-art advances in the computer technology field. Buying each student a $12 textbook explaining how today's computers work minimizes your chances of getting additional instructional materials as technology changes.

Another long-term goal of a computer curriculum is to understand the capabilities and limitations of computer technology in our society. Your curriculum objectives will almost certainly change as computers play a more prominent role in our lives. Today's lesson plans may cover objectives like the effect of computers on our daily lives, the applications for which computers are best suited, and the potentially harmful effects of inappropriately using computers. Even though tomorrow's objectives may be similar, the content of the lessons may be drastically different. As a long-range planner, you need to anticipate these changes and design your curriculum so that you don't become locked into today's content and materials.

What's Important for Teachers to Learn About Computer Technology?

In the short run, you can design staff development activities that respond to the needs of the moment. That is, schools invariably have teachers who are eager to teach and learn about computers. Most school districts can gear up to meet those needs. But, in the long run, what are your expectations for teachers? Should all teachers understand how computer technology works, know the capabilities and limitations of computers, operate and program them, and use computer applications to meet a variety of needs? Or should your expectations vary, depending on the grade, subject level, and interest of the teachers?

The answers to these questions point you toward a long-range staff development plan. As you're responding to the immediate needs expressed by teachers, you need to be laying the foundation for the next several years. After the initial flurry and emotion surrounding computers subsides, you're likely to end up with staff development goals like the following:

- All teachers will have an awareness of how computers work, and their capabilities and limitations in our society. This goal can be achieved even without massive hardware requirements. When teachers have a better understanding of any new technology, they're more receptive to exploration without fear of failure.

- All teachers will learn how to use the talents of computer-proficient students in teaching others. With computers in the homes and computer clubs springing up, it's unrealistic to expect teachers to stay ahead of students who devote considerable energy to this field. Instead, teachers can be taught to capitalize on students' skills, at the same time relieving the pressure of always needing to know more than the student.

- Nonprogramming teachers will learn how to help programming students. Just as in mastering other languages such as French, a person can be conversant in the language without being able to write proficiently in the language. Teachers can be trained to read computer language and spot errors without being programmers themselves. With this skill, teachers and students can work in tandem—each contributing to the learning process.

Whether you adopt these guidelines for staff development or make up your own, you can see from the above examples that it's possible to identify long-range goals for teachers, implementing these goals over time as resources and teacher needs dictate.

THE ROLE OF COMPUTERS IN TOMORROW'S SCHOOLS

If history serves as any predictor, tomorrow's schools won't, at first glance, appear substantially different than today's or yesterday's schools. The teacher will still be the center of instruction. Students will still be taught in groups of about twenty-five. The textbook will still be the dominant medium of instruction. If all of these predictions come true, where will the computer fit in?

Before answering this question, some myths need to be dispelled. First of all, in the next decade we won't see a major revolution in the form and content of schooling as a result of computer technology. In this context, a major revolution means that the teacher shares center stage with the computer as instructor, students are taught in small groups or individually with the computer doing much of the teaching, and the textbook loses its dominant status as the computer becomes recognized as a more powerful teaching medium. To avoid the appearance of being so absolute, the original statement should be amended to read: In the next decade, we won't see a major revolution in the form and content of schooling as a result of computer technology—unless computer technology becomes a national priority for schools, adequate resources flow to districts so that this priority can be implemented, and schools become convinced that this official priority is, in fact, a priority valued by schools.

A second myth assumes that if computers don't live up to their promises, then they have failed. No other innovation in education's history has been lavished with the promotion, propaganda, and preperformance billing as has computer technology's potential in the schools. Even if computers are capable of fulfilling all of the promises of a revolution, they don't have the power to counteract the endless array of forces impinging on their chances for success. Said another way, computer technology can make a major contribution to schooling and still not meet the promises made on its behalf.

A third myth states that improved computer capabilities will lead to more effective and widespread use of computers in schools. "If only computers would get smarter, they would be more helpful." The reality is that these "dumb" computers have far greater potential than our intellect can tap. At present, we simply haven't demonstrated the ability and dedication to push the computer to its limits as an educational tool and teacher.

With these myths exposed for what they are, let's return to the original question: How do computers fit into our schools' future?

From this point forward, computer technology will be a part of our curriculum. Even if we can't say with precision what the curriculum will look like ten years from now, we can say that we need to engage in short-range and long-range planning so tomorrow's adults can begin right now to prepare for a technological world.

Computers will also continue to improve as teachers, primarily because we will improve in our understanding of how to use their potential. Even ten years from now, computer technology may not appear as a teacher in every classroom. Instead, we may see this scarce resource employed in special applications where it politely offers capabilities not available in our human resource pool. Examples of these applications have been cited several times throughout this book, such as special education, simulation activities, and reposition of large volumes of information.

Computer technology will be assigned a variety of management tasks. Within the next few years, computers will appear in virtually all school and central-office settings. With more experience, we will find out that computer technology can save us valuable administrative time and money.

At the beginning of the chapter, we painted an imaginary picture of a major breakthrough in education called the Marcuvian language. In the vignette, the world of the future belonged to those who mastered the Marcuvian language. Today we have a real-life Marcuvian language on our hands in the form of computer technology. Soon this technology will be knocking louder than ever on our schoolhouse doors. The choice will not be whether to invite the computers in. They will come in and they will find a place in our schools. The challenge we face is to anticipate their knock at the door, then answer it with informed, data-based decisions about the speed and shape they take upon entering. In this way, we can channel this powerful resource to provide the best possible education for the students we serve.

REFERENCES CHAPTER 10

Becker, H. J., "Microcomputers in Classrooms: Dreams and Realities," Baltimore, MD: Center for Social Organization of Schools, Johns Hopkins University, Report No. 218, January 1982.

Evans, C., "MicroMillenium," *Science Digest*, June 1981.

Lipson, J. I., "Technology in Science Education: The Next 10 Years," *Computer*, July 1980.

Lopez, A. M., Jr., "Microcomputers: Tools of the Present and Future," *School Media Quarterly*, Spring 1981.

Melmed, A., "Information Technology for U. S. Schools," *Phi Delta Kappan*, Jan. 1982.

Naisbitt, J., *Megatrends: Ten New Directions Transforming Our Lives*, New York: Warner Books, Inc., 1982.

Pritchard, W. H., "Instructional Computing in 2001: A Scenario," *Phi Delta Kappan*, Jan. 1982.

Suppes, P., "The School of the Future: Technological Possibilities," in Rubin, L. (ed.), *The Future of Education: Perspectives on Tomorrow's Schooling*, Boston: Allyn & Bacon, 1975.

INDEX